Manson's
BRISTOL
MISCELLANY

Searching for the soul of the city

Michael Manson

VOLUME 2

 BRISTOL BOOKS   Tangent Books

Bristol Books CIC, The Courtyard,
Wraxall Hill, Wraxall, Bristol, BS48 1NA
www.bristolbooks.org

Tangent Books, Unit 5.16 Paintworks,
Bristol BS4 3EH
www.tangentbooks.co.uk

Manson's Bristol Miscellany: Volume 2
Written and researched by Michael Manson

Published by Bristol Books 2022
in partnership with Tangent Books

ISBN: 9781909446311

Copyright: Michael Manson

Design: Joe Burt

Michael Manson has asserted his right under the Copyright, Designs and Patents Act of 1988 to be
identified as the author of this work.

Any mistakes in this book are entirely the author's responsibility.
The author would be happy to correct them in any future prints of this book.

INTRODUCTION

Welcome to *Manson's Bristol Miscellany* Volume 2.

The *Bristol Miscellany* was originally conceived as one book, but grew into two. Volume 1 covers: Bristol's early days; power and politics; business and trade; markets and fairs; the slave trade; law and order; public protest; Bristol's mines; plagues and public health, and so much more.

This volume looks at: transport and communications; the arts; housing and homelessness and the architecture of Bristol. Many of these topics are not just history but live issues today.

I initially started writing the *Bristol Miscellany* in the 2000s when articles were serialised in the now defunct *Bristol Review of Books*. The 2020 Covid 19 lockdown gave me the impetus to complete the project.

Self-isolation for four months in early 2020 provided time to research, reflect and work on the text. In the summer of 2020, as restrictions eased, I ventured out and explored. I inspected buildings and sought new views across the city. It was a liberation to revisit Bristol's parks and follow brooks.

Then, in June 2020, something not entirely unexpected happened. During a Black Lives Matters demonstration Edward Colston's statue in the city centre was pulled down, rolled along the waterfront and dumped in the docks. (See Volume 1 for information on Colston). Suddenly, Bristol's history was on the world stage.

The re-evaluation of the Colston myth was long overdue.

I remember writing about Colston 30 years before in my book *Bristol Beyond the Bridge* (Redcliffe Press, 1988). I was astounded that such a man could be so widely venerated. Three years ago I visited one of the slave trading 'castles' on the Cape Coast of Ghana. It was a moment of deep epiphany. As I stood in a dark dungeon starring at a narrow door, the gateway of no return, I asked myself, why on earth would we celebrate anybody who was involved in this vast genocide?

There is much to celebrate in Bristol's past – but not this.

The toppling of the statue demonstrated how our understanding and interpretation of history can shift with time. Our relationship with the past is not static. Heroes can become villains, villains can become heroes.

Subsequently, the *'We are Bristol' History Commission* found that 80 per cent of Bristolians said that the Colston Statue should remain on display in a horizontal position with graffiti intact, in a Bristol Museum.[1]

History isn't just about heroes and villains – but everyday people. As I wrote in my introduction to Volume 1, I'd be delighted if the *Miscellany* helps readers see their environment a little more clearly - even embark on their own voyage of discovery. Opening your eyes to history can make the world look different. Bristol is a very special place. Let's keep it that way.

Michael Manson

---

1   The Colston Statue: What Next? 'We are Bristol' History Commission Full Report. 4 February 2022.

TRAINS, TRAMS, BOATS AND PLANES

TRAVELLING AT UNIMAGINABLE SPEED

- God's Wonderful Railway -

On 31 August 1840, excitable passengers climbed aboard open-top carriages for the first journey from Bristol to Bath along Isambard Kingdom Brunel's (1806-59) wide gauge Great Western Railway.[1] Thousands of spectators watched with awe as the steaming *Fire-Ball* thundered down the line. Within 15 minutes of leaving Temple Meads Station the train had reached Keynsham. After a two minute stop it was on its way again. It was travelling at an unimaginable speed. The 20mph velocity was exhilarating. Some

Temple Meads Station. GWR terminus (left), Bristol and Exeter line (centre). © Bristol Culture (Bristol Museum & Art Gallery).

Temple Meads Station. In the distance, the Jacobean-style Bristol and Exeter railway office of 1852.
© Bristol Culture (Bristol Museum & Art Gallery).

passengers even feared the rapidity of the motion would be harmful to their health. In all, the journey to Bath took 32 minutes.

The railway age was underway, though it would be a further six months before the 119 mile route to Paddington was opened.

Meanwhile, the Bristol and Exeter line, run by a different company, but with the omnipresent Brunel as engineer, was completed in 1844. It also had its terminus at Temple Meads – placed at a right-angle to Brunel's passenger shed.

The concept of a *rail way* was nothing new in Bristol. Since 1832, coal had been transported by wagons on iron tracks, the Dram Way, from the Kingswood Coal field down to a wharf at Keynsham – a distance of 5½ miles.[2] But the steam train turned the world

upside-down. By reducing the time and cost of travel the railways gave an enormous boost to Bristol's trade and industry.

Temple Meads Railway Station wasn't best placed. Ideally, a train station should be centrally located. In Bristol, a terminus adjacent to the docks would have been the preferred option. But Bristol's hilly topography limited the options. In the end, Temple Meads was the nearest undeveloped land available. And just as important, the land was owned by the Bristol Corporation who was keen to sell.[3]

In 1861 there was a proposal to nudge the passenger railway station further into the city. There was a plan for a central terminus in Queen Square, and from there a new branch line would extend to the lower slopes of Brandon Hill.[4] Alarm at the appropriation of public open spaces, together with the fear of damage by fire to houses and shipping meant the idea was fiercely opposed and subsequently dropped. A year later, another unsuccessful proposal was put forward, this time, with a grand terminus built over a covered-up River Frome (as it is today) at Narrow Quay.[5]

Nevertheless, the arrival of the GWR unleashed a burst of industrial hyperactivity. Brunel set the example. Civil engineering on such a scale could be done! 'The greatest public work ever constructed' claimed Arrowsmith's 1906 *Dictionary of Bristol*. The trains were as much for the transport of goods as for passengers. In just 20 years Bristol's trade hinterland expanded beyond recognition. Soon Bristol was connected by rail to Gloucester, Birmingham (just about!), Cardiff and Exeter. Smaller lines crossed the city to Avonmouth, Portishead and Fishponds.

The roads between Temple Meads station and Bristol Bridge became so congested that a new thoroughfare, Victoria Street, had to be built.

'A third-class passenger in 1908 has the choice of numerous trains; he travels in luxury compared with his predecessors; he can reach London in two hours' smooth running, and enjoy an excellent luncheon on the way.'[6]

There was no lack of investors – money was to be made from railways. This enthusiasm for the railways has been described as a 'feverish mania'[7]. Bristol's business people could see the wider opportunities for the distribution of their wares. The railways became the beating heart of Victorian Bristol. Bristol's major industries – chocolate, tobacco and packaging – employing thousands of people, were spurred into action. Life moved at a faster pace – the streets of Bristol were crowded with wagons,

drays and carters moving goods to and from the stations and yards. Within 20 years, the roads leading from the station to Bristol Bridge became so congested with traffic that a new thoroughfare, Victoria Street, 'with every conceivable style of architecture', was cut through the old and run-down residential area of Temple and St Thomas.[8]

The fields of Temple Meads and St Philips disappeared under acres of goods yards. Even the serenity of the Cathedral was disturbed by the letting-off of steam and the clanking of shunted wagons from neighbouring Canon's Marsh.

There was the difficulty of the gauge, however. Brunel had insisted on the 7ft ¼ inch broad gauge, which he claimed allowed a faster and smoother ride.[9] He didn't see it as a problem, asserting that the GWR would never have any connections with other main lines. How wrong he was. For example, goods going from Bristol to Birmingham had to be unloaded at Gloucester, where the broad gauge ended, and then reloaded onto a standard gauge (4ft 8 ½ in) train. This was one of the few battles that Brunel was to lose. The GWR capitulated and under government pressure, bit by bit, they reluctantly converted their lines to standard gauge. This painfully slow process was completed by 1892.

Nevertheless, the energy was palpable. Teams of navvies – nomadic labourers – were everywhere. Bristol's landscape was newly sculpted by railway cuttings, embankments, bridges and viaducts. Recently built villas next to Whiteladies Road had to be demolished to make way for the Clifton Extension Railway.[10] A mile-long tunnel was then dug under Durdham Down to extend the line to Avonmouth. The hill to the east of Ashley Vale – now called Narroways – was carved up like a hot-cross-bun. St Mary Redcliffe lost part of its churchyard when a tunnel for the Docks Railway was bored under Redcliffe Hill.

Of course, there was another side to the coin. Within three years of the opening of the GWR to London all horse drawn coaches from Bristol to the capital had ceased. Market towns

For all its faults Temple Meads remains Bristol's core train station.

such as Marshfield on the Gloucestershire border were by-passed. The once hectic 18th century coaching inns, with their wide arched entrances and busy stables, fell silent. The landscape of the country was forever changed.

For all its faults Temple Meads remains Bristol's core train station. Today, however, Brunel's splendid Victorian gothic engine shed is used as an exhibition space, while his offices are occupied by an 'innovation and incubation centre'.

- Bristol's Railways -

By the beginning of the 20th century a confusing network of branch lines ran through and around Bristol.

The Clifton Extension Line was initially built to create a link between Temple Meads and Clifton (Clifton Down) via Montpelier and Redland. A further extension to Avonmouth required a mile long-tunnel to be dug under Durdham Down.

The Bristol and South Wales Union Railway originally involved a steam ferry crossing of the Severn until a tunnel was built under the river – opened in 1885. Stations along the line included Ashley

Hill, Bonnington Road (Horfield) and Filton. (A new station, Abbey Wood, serving the nearby Ministry of Defence offices, opened south of the original Filton Station in 1996.)

The Bristol and Portishead Pier and Railway opened in 1867. This line travelled in a wide sweep through Bedminster and then took a spectacular journey along the Avon Gorge and under the Suspension Bridge. Between 1928 and 1932 there was a halt at the bottom of Nightingale Valley for visitors to Leigh Woods. There were also 'football specials' stopping at Ashton Gate Station – opened in 1906. The line was closed for passengers in 1964, though there are plans to re-open as part of the MetroWest transport scheme.

The Bristol Habour Junction Railway connected the docks to the main lines. For goods only, it opened in 1872. A tunnel was dug under St Mary Redcliffe and Redcliffe Hill emerging at Bathurst Basin. Part of the churchyard was destroyed. It closed in 1964.

The Bristol & North Somerset Railway was primarily intended for transporting coal from the North Somerset coalfield. Its station at Brislington – opened in 1873 – was also used for commuting into Bristol and Bath. Brislington Station was closed for passengers in 1959 and closed for goods in 1963.

Henbury Loop Line of the GWR. The Filton to Avonmouth Railway provided a direct route to Avonmouth Docks. It was intended for freight but also, at times, carried passengers.

The Midland Railway opened a small branch line in 1870 that served 'Fish Ponds' (Now the site of Safeway supermarket.) and Staple Hill. Terminating at St Philips, the line closed for passengers in 1953 and for goods in 1967.

Bristol Port Railway and Pier. Initially unconnected to the wider network, this six mile line was principally a passenger service, carrying workers and holiday makers between Hotwells and Avonmouth. Hotwells Station, a short walk from Clifton Rocks Railway, opened in 1864. In 1885, the Clifton Extension Railway line to Avonmouth joined the BPR&P at Sneyd Park Junction. The BPR&P closed in 1921 with the building of the Portway.

Timetabling was a nightmare. No

Clifton Down Railway Station, 1908.

wonder, in 1924, most of these lines were merged to come under the umbrella of the Great Western Railway. In 1947 the 'Big Four' regional railways, which included GWR, were nationalised by the post-war Labour government. On 1 January 1948 GWR became the Western Region of British Railways.

In 1963 Dr Richard Beeching (1913-85) produced his controversial, and arguably short-sighted, report *The Reshaping of British Railways*. In the following years several less profitable stations in Bristol were closed.

In the 1970s and 80s, as rail freight decreased, redundant goods yards were sold by British Rail, releasing a considerable amount of land. The sale of these drab acres of inner-city terrain played a large part in Bristol's 1990s economic regeneration. Developments in Canon's Marsh, Temple Gate and St Philips were all on old railway sidings and goods yards, while Clifton Down Shopping Centre was built above the coal yard of Clifton Down Station.

In the 21st century, as proposals are put forward for a Bristol underground, perhaps it's time to consider if some of the lost stations could be reinstated.

TIME TRAVEL

- Bristol time -

In 1841, passengers arriving at Temple Meads Station from London would notice that their pocket watches were wrong. If they checked against the station clock they would discover their watch was 10½ minutes fast. What had happened? Was the train a time travel machine?

The arrival of the GWR railway had some unforeseen effects. One of these was the changing of Bristol's time.

Until the 1880s there was no standard time in England. Each town kept its own time, calculated by the height of the sun, and signalled by church bells. Before the age of mass communication this discrepancy caused few problems. It was only with the arrival of the railway in Bristol in 1841 that matters got confusing. For the railways ran on London time. Thus the noon train from Bristol left Temple Meads at 11.49 am.

After many missed trains the Bristol Corporation attempted to clarify matters by putting an extra second hand on the Corn Exchange clock.[11] It only added to the confusion.

In 1852, Bristol bowed to the inevitable and accepted Greenwich Meantime as the standard for the city.

It would be another 30 years, however, until this approach was adopted nationally. The clock on the Corn Exchange still has three hands – with the extra hand showing Bristol time. This third hand is, however, a recent addition added by the Temple Local History Group in the 1980s.

'THE POLICE SHOULD STOP IT'

- Trams -

When it was first proposed that a tram line should run from the centre of Bristol to the Downs there was a shudder of concern from some of the more faint-hearted Clifton residents. Would property prices plummet? Would the Downs be over-run by undesirable visitors? One Clifton resident wrote satirically (I hope!) to the *Bristol Mercury*:

'...it is something terrible and most wicked that the disgusting tramway is to bring the nasty, low inhabitants of Bristol up to our region...' The sarcastic correspondent finished by demanding that 'the police should stop it'.[12]

Nevertheless, in 1875, Bristol's first tram, a double-decker carriage running on iron rails drawn by two horses, made its inaugural journey from Perry Road, along Queens Road and Whiteladies Road, to its terminus by St John's Church, Apsley Road. Despite the initial reservations, this new mode of transport was soon deemed a popular and, indeed, profitable business.[13] So much so that in its first year investors in the Bristol Tramways Company received an impressive 15% per annum dividend on their investment.[14]

Before long a web of tram routes spread to the suburbs from what was soon to be called the Tramway Centre at St Augustine's Parade.[15]

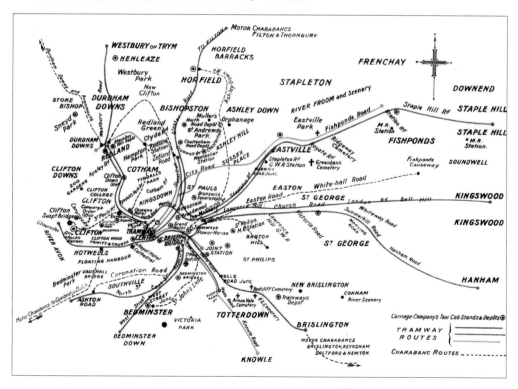

A web of tram routes radiated from the Tramway Centre at St Augustine's Parade to the suburbs.

By 1900, trams were powered from a generating station by St Philip's Bridge.

There were trams to Eastville, St George, Ashley Hill, Horfield, Hotwells, Bedminster and Totterdown.

The unwanted trams were pushed into an overgrown wasteland, stripped of their iron and unceremoniously torched.

A number of horse buses continued to operate from cab stands for shorter journeys. These were discontinued in 1906 and replaced by motor omnibuses, also operated by the Tramway Company.

By 1916 Bristol trams were carrying over 60 million passengers a year. It was now possible to take shopping trips to town, enjoy music hall entertainment at the Palace Theatre in Old Market or – God help the people of Clifton! – make excursions to the Downs. For many, these rattling double-decker vehicles, adorned in advertising boards, had opened-up a whole new world.

The Bristol Tramways and Carriage Company, as it was now called, was eventually acquired by the Bristol Corporation in 1937. From that date trams were gradually replaced by the quieter and more flexible green Bristol omnibuses.

There is a sad postscript to the history of Bristol's trams. The final end of the trams came suddenly and permanently. St Philip's Bridge, next to the Temple Back generating station,

Brislington Tram Depot, 1908.

was bombed during the 1941 Good Friday air raid.[18] The bridge carried the main electricity cable that powered the trams. The trams were never to run again.

Rather than being salvaged, the trams were taken on one last journey and towed to the Kingswood depot. Here, a rough hole was knocked through the back wall of the depot's brick shed. The trams were then pushed into overgrown wasteland, stripped of their iron and unceremoniously torched. Not one of those handsome Bristol electric trams remains.[19]

Miraculously, one of the original tram depots remains substantially unchanged. The imposing Brislington Depot gatehouse was modelled, in keeping with Arnos Court (see page 125) directly across the road, on an 18th century stable block. The entrance hides the plainer sheds behind, where the trams were stored and maintained. The building is now used as a storehouse for council vehicles and was briefly set up as temporary morgue – thankfully not needed – during the 2020-21 Covid pandemic.

Brislington Tram Depot gatehouse was modelled, in keeping with Arnos Court directly across the road, on an 18th century stable block.

A PASSAGE TO JAMAICA

- Passenger steamships -

Unlike Southampton or Liverpool, Bristol was never a major centre of passenger embarkation. Despite Brunel's vision of interconnected travel from London by train, which included an overnight stay at the Royal Western Hotel (now Brunel House behind City Hall) and then steamship to New York, things never quite worked out like that.

Even so, smaller passenger vessels did leave the port, while freight ships would take the occasional traveller.

The Bank Holiday Act of 1871 officially confirmed that employees were entitled to (unpaid) days off work.[20] Shilling (5p) return train trips to the seaside – invariably Weston-super-Mare with its clean air and two mile stretch of golden sands (and its equally vast stretch of foreshore mud) – became increasingly popular.

Pleasure steamers also offered recreational trips along the Bristol Channel. During the 1870s a surprising number of white funnelled paddle steamers were to be seen scudding up and down and across the Channel's difficult waters. The white funnels belonged to the Scottish owned Campbell Line, the largest operator of steamers in the Channel. During the summer months of 1872, steamers sailed daily (weather permitting) from Portishead Pier to Ilfracombe and Lynmouth.[21]

The Edwardian age of luxury was not confined to transatlantic liners. For just one day, you could dress up in your finest clothes and experience the splendour of the elegant saloons and splendid wood-panelled dining rooms serving fresh salmon; all the while gliding down the Bristol Channel with sublime views of the coast from either side of the deck. In 1911 there was even a daily steamer, leaving the Bathurst Basin, sailing via the Cut, for Cardiff.

By the beginning of the 20th century Campbell's had 13 Bristol Channel steamers operating in the summer.[22]

For longer journeys the Bristol Steam Navigation Company sailed to Cork and Dublin twice a week, and to Antwerp every ten days. Additionally, there was the opportunity to take passages to Jamaica, North America and even Australia. In 1910, the *Royal Edward* boasted it was the fastest passenger steamer on the

PORTISHEAD PIER

BRISTOL CHANNEL,

IN CONNECTION WITH THE

GREAT WESTERN, MIDLAND, BRISTOL AND EXETER, AND **BRISTOL & PORTISHEAD RAILWAYS.**

STEAMERS SAIL FROM PORTISHEAD PIER

(WEATHER PERMITTING), FOR

ILFRACOMBE AND LYNMOUTH

Daily during June, July, August, September and October.

CORK

Every Tuesday, Thursday, and Friday throughout the year.

THE SAME STEAMERS LEAVE

ILFRACOMBE.	CORK.
Daily throughout the same.	Every Monday, Tuesday, & Friday

Steamers also call (weather permitting) at or off PORTISHEAD PIER on their voyages from Bristol to Bideford, Barnstaple, Cardiff, Carmarthen, Dublin, Hayle, Ilfracombe, Liverpool, Newport, Neath, Padstow, Swansea, Tenby, Waterford and Wexford about one hour and a half after leaving Bristol, and if required land Passengers at the Pier on their return voyages to meet the Up Trains, avoiding the delays by tide, the tedious voyages up the river Avon, and inconvenience of Passengers and their Luggage being conveyed from Cumberland Basin to the Midland, Great Western, and Bristol and Exeter Railway Stations.
Tickets at low fares are issued at all the principal Stations on the above-named Railways for the through journey to Cork, and to Lynmouth Lynton, and Ilfracombe, via Portishead, inclusive of all expenses.
Constant communication with vessels in the roadstead.
First-class Hotel accomodation at the Pier.

Pleasure steamers offered recreational trips along the Bristol Channel.

Canadian Route, completing the journey from Bristol to Quebec in five days and 20 hours. 'Under four days open sea passage.' The Atlantic Ocean Service in conjunction with the Canadian Pacific Railway ran ships in the summer months from Avonmouth to Montreal and Quebec. There was accommodation for a limited number of passengers, 'male only, at saloon rates'.[23]

A day out on a Bristol Channel steamer remained a popular excursion right up until the Second World War. But after the war the experience was never quite the same. Reduced maintenance standards due to hard financial times took a toll on the look of the boat and the quality of the experience. Campbell's White Funnel fleet was showing its age and in 1958 the company went into receivership.[24]

Cargo ships would also take passengers. 1921.

MV Balmoral

The MV Balmoral, was launched from Southampton in 1949. Built by Thorneycroft and Company Ltd, it is the sole survivor of the Campbell fleet. As well as operating around the Bristol Channel, the Balmoral has been used as an Isle of Wight ferry, for mini cruises to the Sicily Isles and as an ill-fated restaurant/disco in Dundee. At time of publication it is laid up in Bristol harbour undergoing restoration. www.thebalmoral.org.uk.

- *The Sailor's friend* -

Samuel Plimsoll

Samuel Plimsoll (1824-98) was born in Colston Parade, in the shadow of St Mary Redcliffe Church. After tireless campaigning, the Shipping Acts of 1875 and 1876 introduced the Plimsoll Line, a mark drawn on all cargo ships indicating the maximum depth to which they can be safely loaded. This simple, yet effective, measure has saved many lives.

The rubber soled Plimsoll deck shoes – which in Bristol we call 'daps' – are also named after him.

TO THE SKY AND BEYOND

- Bristol's aircraft industry -

The British and Colonial Airplane Company Limited was established in Bristol in 1910, one year after Louis Bleriot (1872-1936) became the first person to fly across the English Channel by plane.

In 1909, while on holiday in France, Sir George White (1854-1916), the avuncular chairman of the Bristol Tramways Company, witnessed a flying display by the American Wilbur Wright (1867-1912). 'We must start an aircraft company', he cabled his brother, Samuel.[25]

On return, Sir George requisitioned dusty tram sheds at Filton and gathered together a team of skilled craftsmen to build his first flying machine, the *Zodiac*. It was a complete flop and never got off the ground. But they learnt from their mistakes. The frame of the next aircraft was exquisitely crafted out of spruce, ash and walnut; the wings were covered in strong but flexible Egyptian cotton cloth.[26]

In 1910, spectators gathered on the Downs to wonder at the miracle of a heavier-than-air flying machine. They had expected an elevation of just a few feet but were astounded when the *Bristol Boxkite* – it really was just a large kite with an engine attached – soared like a bird 45 metres over their heads. The *Boxkite*, clearly modelled on the French Farman Biplane, was a commercial triumph. A new industry for Bristol was born. The outbreak of the First World War consolidated the demand for aircraft. At that stage aeroplanes were

The *Bristol Boxkite* soared like a bird. A new industry for Bristol was born.

used for aerial reconnaissance rather than as weapons of war.[27]

It is an unfortunate truth that aviation development has invariably been led by military needs. By 1914, at the start of the First World War, over 400 people were employed at Filton building bi-planes for the Royal Flying Corps.[28] In 1920, the company was renamed the Bristol Aeroplane Company.

From modest beginnings Bristol has become a hub for the world's aviation industry. Bombers, commercial aircraft, fighter planes, helicopters and guided weapons have all been manufactured at Filton. Aerospace and its related businesses is a major feature of Bristol's economy, employing thousands of people, generating billions of pounds revenue.

Britannia

- Some Bristol-built commercial aeroplanes -

Bristol Brabazon (1949)

When it was first flown this massive eight-engine plane, built by the Bristol Aeroplane Company Ltd, was the biggest aircraft in the world. The Filton runway had to be extended so that it could take-off and land. In the process the neighbouring village of Charlton was demolished. A technical success, but an economic disaster, the *Brabazon*, never went into production.

Britannia (1952)

The 'whispering giant', a blend of jet and propeller propulsion, was built for long haul 'Empire routes'. Its beginnings were not auspicious. A test flight ended in the Severn mud. In 1957, a later prototype crashed into woods (later named Britannia Wood) near Overdale Road, Downend. All 14 on board were killed, though nobody on the ground was hurt.

In spite of these early mishaps, 85 *Britannias* were built. They proved to be safe and robust planes.

Concorde (1969)

The seemingly impossible dream of supersonic passenger travel was realised, a fine example of European cooperation. The French insisted on the 'e' in *Concorde*.

The final flight in 2003 over Bristol of *Concorde Alfa Foxtrot*, like a great white bird heading to the knacker's yard, brought a tear to many a Bristolian's eye.

Aerospace Bristol *is a fascinating museum dedicated to all things flying, with George White's horse drawn tram also thrown in.*

THE LOCATION WAS FAR FROM IDEAL

- The first Bristol airport -

Bristol International Airport, seven miles outside Bristol along the A38 at Lulsgate, is an important departure and arrival point for West of England travellers. Yet Bristol's airport was once much closer to the city centre.

Bristol's first airport, only the third municipal airport in the country, was established in 1929.

Fully alive to the commercial opportunities, the Corporation purchased 260 acres of land, 'within three miles from Temple Meads Station'[29]. The plot of land was sufficient for a 1,000 yard runway. One small matter: the boundaries of Bristol had to be changed to accommodate the new airport within its jurisdiction.

Bristol Corporation, which had no experience of running an airport, accepted an offer by Bristol Aeroplane Club to manage the site. They were able to boast one full-time engineer whose duty it was 'to certify and inspect each machine each day'.[30] The future King, Prince George, officially opened the airport on 31 May 1930.

Flights included a twice-daily air service to Splott Airport in

Cardiff. (These were the days before a Severn Bridge: the trip to Cardiff via the Aust Ferry could take hours.) The fare was not cheap: eight shillings for a single flight; 12 shillings return (£0.60p). Other flights were available to Bournemouth. Eventually, an overseas service was offered to Paris and fashionable Le Touquet on the north coast of France.

During the Second World War the airport was viewed as a safer departure point than London's main airport at Croydon. It was subsequently requisitioned by the Air Ministry and used for flights to Ireland and neutral Portugal. In 1940, Queen Wilhelmina of the Netherlands (1890-1948), hastily fleeing from her mother country, arrived wearing plimsolls and had no luggage but her sponge bag.[31]

Celebrities who secretly passed through Whitchurch included Winston Churchill (1874-

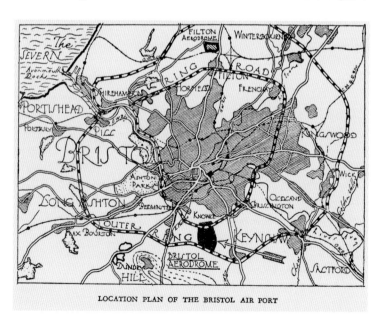

LOCATION PLAN OF THE BRISTOL AIR PORT

Bristol's first airport was established in 1929. The boundaries of Bristol had to be changed to accommodate the new airport within its jurisdiction.

Bristol Airport at Whitchurch was able to boast one full-time engineer whose duty it was 'to certify and inspect each machine each day'.

1965), Bob Hope (1903-2003) and the star of *Gone with the Wind*, Leslie Howard (1893-1943). Tragically, the plane carrying Howard was shot down over the Bay of Biscay – no one survived. Mystery surrounds the loss of this BOAC plane in neutral airspace. Declassified papers relating to the incident were inexplicably resealed until 2025.

In retrospect, the location of Whitchurch airport was far from ideal. Pilots were alarmed by the hazard posed by the runway's proximity to the 800ft Dundry Hill, topped by its distinctive church tower. The airport was consequently transferred in 1957 to the former RAF airfield at Lulsgate Bottom.

Boasting 'a sun terrace overlooking the airfield' the new airport became a destination in its own right.

While the Lulsgate site had a runway double the length of that at Whitchurch it, nevertheless, had its own drawback being particularly prone to early morning mist causing flights to be delayed or diverted.

Part of the original Whitchurch runway is still visible today; a popular spot for dog walkers and joy riders. The remainder is buried under Hengrove Retail and Leisure Park.

'Wo sind wir?'

The first aircraft to use the runway of the newly enlarged Lulsgate airfield, then called Broadfield Down, was a German bomber. The plane's navigator had lost his bearings and assumed he was flying over France. After landing on the airstrip the confused pilot shouted to workmen, 'Where are we?'

Realising that he had landed in enemy territory the pilot immediately attempted to take off. He was only stopped by a mechanical digger being dumped in front of the aircraft. Soldiers, attached to the airfield, took the crew prisoners. The aircraft, a new Junkers 88, with all the latest technology, was a prized capture.[32]

A STEEP ROLLER-COASTER INCLINE

- Temple Gate flyover -

The single lane temporary flyover at Temple Gate was an efficient and enjoyable piece of traffic engineering. © Bristol Post.

This much loved single lane temporary flyover at Temple Gate was an efficient and enjoyable piece of traffic engineering. Cyclists were banned, a prohibition that was often ignored by the more adventurous. The second-hand steel structure was purchased from Coventry in 1968 and was in use until 1997.

For many, in simpler times, it was a childhood treat. 'A steep roller coaster incline and then, at the top, when you were within touching distance of the Grosvenor Hotel and it seemed as if you were about to crash into a third floor bedroom, there was a sharp right turn followed by a stomach twisting drop to Redcliffe Way. Such fun.'

Several traffic layouts have been put into service at Temple Gate since, but none has been as effective as this 30-year-old 'temporary' solution.

ENDNOTES

1   Aughton, P., *Bristol – A People's History,* 2003, Carnegie Publishing, pp.172-5.
2   Buchanan, R.A., *The Industrial Archaeology of Bristol,* 1967, Bristol Branch of the Historical Association, p.6.
3   Malpass, P., *The Making of Victorian Bristol,* 2019, The Boydell Press, p.158.
4   Latimer, J. *Annals of Nineteenth Century Bristol,* 1897, W. & F. Morgan. p.388.
5   ibid., p.393-4.
6   Stone, G.F., *Bristol As It Was and As It Is,* 1909, Walter Reid, p.80.
7   Briggs, A., *A Social History of England,* 1983, Weidenfeld and Nicolson, p.210.
8   Manson, M., *Bristol Beyond the Bridge,* 1988, Redcliffe Press, p.93.
9   Buchanan, R.A. & Williams, M., *Brunel's Bristol,* 1982, Redcliffe Press, p.36.
10 Malpass, P., op. cit., p.171.
11 Latimer, J., op. cit., p.253.
12 Harvey, C. & Press, J., *Studies in the Business History of Bristol,* 1988, Bristol Academic Press, p.145.
13 ibid., p.145.
14 *Arrowsmith's Dictionary of Bristol,* 1906, p.403.
15 Harvey, C. & Press, J., op. cit., p.142.
16 *Arrowsmith's Dictionary of Bristol,* 1906, p.404.
17 ibid., p.404.
18 Warne, F.G., *Bristol Bombed,* 1943, F.G. Warne, p.12.
19 A horse drawn Bristol tram can be viewed, rather incongruously, at the Aerospace Bristol Museum.
20 Briggs, A., op. cit., p. 214.
21 Jennings, H. J., *The Bristol Guide including Clifton,* 1872. R.W. Bingham.
22 Anon, *Balmoral and the story of the Bristol Channel Steamers,* 1992, Waverley Excursions Ltd, p.7.
23 Baker. J., *The New Guide to Bristol and Clifton,* 1912, J Baker & Sons, p.274.
24 Anon, *Balmoral and the story of the Bristol Channel Steamers,* 1992, Waverley Excursions Ltd, p.13.
25 Bolton, D., *Made in Bristol,* 2011, Redcliffe, p.20.
26 Pudney, J. *Bristol Fashion,* 1960, Putnam, p.16.
27 Ibid., p.70.
28 Stone, G., *Rearmament, War and the Performance of the Bristol Aeroplane Company in Harvey, C. and Press, J., Studies in the Business History of Bristol,* 1988, Bristol Academic Press, p.186.
29 Abercrombie, P. & Brueton, B., *Bristol and Bath Regional Planning Scheme,* 1930, University Press Liverpool, p.110.
30 ibid., p.111.
31 Broda, C., *Symes Avenue: Building on the Past,* 2008, p38.
32 https://www.bbc.co.uk/history/ww2peopleswar/stories/60/a5382560. shtml 26 April 2020.

GETTING AROUND

SO MANY BRIDGES TO CROSS

- Bristol's bridges -

Bristol Bridge. The first stone structure, a four arched bridge with shops on either side, was opened in 1247.

Bristol owes its existence to its bridge. The name Bristol is a corruption of the old English word Brigstowe – first mentioned in 1063 – meaning place by the bridge. The first Bristol Bridge, a wooden structure, was probably built around this time.

Bristol is justifiably known for Isambard Kingdom Brunel's masterpiece, Clifton Suspension Bridge. While Clifton Suspension Bridge may be world famous there are other bridges in Bristol of more importance transport-wise. Somebody once claimed that there are more bridges in Bristol than in Venice – while this may be well off-the-mark, there are a surprising number. In fact, depending on how you count them, there are 18 across the Avon and the Cut and 17 across the Floating Harbour

Castle Bridge (2017) links Finzel's Reach to Castle Park.

and the Feeder. And that's not including the railway bridges.

In some ways the Clifton Suspension Bridge is merely a decorative bauble; the city could function quite well without it. But close St Philip's Causeway or the Cumberland Basin Plimsoll Bridge and the city grinds to a standstill.

A rash of bridge building was necessitated by the digging of the New Cut (1803-06). The Cut, a man-made channel that diverted the Avon, facilitated the establishment of the Floating Harbour. Within the space of a couple of years Bristol had three new bridges: Prince Street Bridge; Bedminster Bridge and Bath Road Bridge.

Since then additional bridges have been added intermittently – either due to the pressures of traffic or sometimes to commemorate an event. Indeed, in the last 30 years or so, a handful of new bridges have been added to the cityscape: St Philip's Marsh Spine Road bridge (1994) (technically two

bridges); Pero's Bridge (1999) spanning St Augustine's Reach; Temple Quay's serpentine Valentine Bridge (2001), the stainless steel 'cheese grater' bridge (2008) at Temple Quay Central and Castle Bridge (2017) linking Castle Park with the Finzel's Reach development.

There are also new bridges that allow pedestrians and cyclists to progress alongside the harbour without having to make detours. The turquoise Poole's Wharf Bridge (commissioned 1991) spans the entrance to Poole's Wharf Marina, while the Bathurst Basin footbridge (1985), opposite the Ostrich pub, replaces a former railway bridge.

There's still room for more bridges. There is on-going discussion about a bridge across the widest part of the docks linking the SS Great Britain and Hotwells Road. The next time the city has something to commemorate maybe we should celebrate by building a bridge. Anyone for a new bridge in 2023 to celebrate the 750th anniversary of the formation of the County of Bristol?

SOME OF BRISTOL'S BRIDGES

- Across the Frome -

Wickham Bridge. Wickham Glen, Stapleton. Built of pennant stone in the early 17th century, this is Bristol's oldest surviving bridge. Wickham Bridge was on the old road to Gloucester. There was probably a medieval bridge on this site.

- Across the Avon Floating Harbour[1] -

Bristol Bridge. The first stone structure, a four arched bridge, built along the lines of the old London Bridge, was opened in 1247. There were shops lining either side of the bridge and in the middle it was spanned by a chantry dedicated to the Assumption of Our Lady. The chantry was charged with the upkeep of the bridge 'against the ravages of the sea ebbing and flowing daily under the same'.[2] With time the bridge became too small and overcrowded. 'Last Wednesday, a man had his leg broke on the bridge by the wheel of a wagon going over it.'[3] The new bridge, opened in 1769, is substantially the bridge we have today, though it was widened in 1873.

Cumberland Basin Flyover (Plimsoll Bridge). A swing bridge on a central pivot. It was built between 1962-65 as part of the Cumberland Basin development. It replaced Brunel's distinctive tubular swing lock bridges (1844-48) which remain in the shadow of the newer structure.

Pero's Bridge. Pero Jones (1753-88) was a slave-servant to John Pinney (1740-1818), sugar merchant and plantation owner. The horned bridge, opened in 1999, was designed by Irish sculptor Eilis O'Connell in conjunction with engineers Ove Arup & Partners. It commemorates, and pays tribute to, all the Africans and West Indians enslaved by Bristol's merchants and planters. This 'sculpture you

Wickham Bridge, Stapleton, was on the old road to Gloucester. There was probably a medieval bridge on this site.

Redcliffe Bridge (1941) operates like a giant seesaw using counterweights.

could walk across' was built to link Queen Square with the newly developed Canon's Marsh.

Prince Street Bridge. The first bridge here was built in 1809 replacing the ancient Gibb Ferry. The current swing bridge was installed in 1879.

Redcliffe Bridge. The only bascule road bridge in the city. The bridge operates like a seesaw using counterweights. (Bascule is French for rocker.) It was one of the few civil engineering works to be undertaken in Bristol during the

Second World War (1939-45). Opened in 1941, it was part of the misguided transport scheme that saw a road, now thankfully removed, cutting across Queen Square.

St Philip's Bridge. Also known as the Ha'penny Bridge – a reference to the toll originally charged for crossing. It was built, with a drawbridge in its centre, in 1841, replacing the Counterslip Ferry. In 1876, a more substantial structure was built. The current bridge was constructed after its predecessor was destroyed in April 1941 by a direct hit by a bomb during the Bristol blitz.

- Across the Avon New Cut -

Temple Island Bridge. The bridge that leads nowhere. This footbridge (2019) was designed to connect St Philips to the Bristol Arena. The Arena was conceived by Bristol's first elected mayor, George Ferguson (b.1947) but was subsequently scrapped by Ferguson's successor Marvin Rees (b. 1972). The bridge will hopefully be incorporated into Bristol University's new Temple Quarter Campus.

Ashton Swing Bridge. Opened in 1906. Unique in Bristol, this was once a double-decker swing bridge with a road above and railway below. In 2016/7 the lower level was refurbished to accommodate the MetroBus, as well as walkers and cyclists. The control cabin no longer exists.

Bath Road Bridge (sometimes called Hill Bridge). An accident-prone site. The initial structure collapsed on the point of completion in 1806, killing two workmen. The bridge collapsed for a second time in 1855, when an out-of-control Cardiff steam barge crashed

into it.

'The vessel had conveyed a cargo of coke to the railway works and was returning down the river, in which there was a strong current, when through unskillful management, it struck the ribs of the bridge with great violence. The effect was instantaneous, the structure collapsing, according to the expression of an eyewitness, like a child's house of cards' [4]

Unique in Bristol, Ashton Swing Bridge was a double-decker bridge with a road above and railway below. In 2016/7 the lower level was refurbished to accommodate the MetroBus.

Not a vestige was left standing, and the carts and passengers crossing at the time were thrown into the river. Two persons lost their lives, one being a wagoner whose cart was found next day below Rownham.

The Bath Road Bridge was replaced yet again in 1909.

Bedminster Bridge. Opened in 1807, the original bridge, called Harford's Bridge, was built to cross the newly dug Cut. To cope with the increased demands of traffic it was replaced in 1884.

Goal Bridge Ferry. This footbridge replaced the Goal Ferry which was operating until 1935. It is one of Bristol's four suspension bridges.

Langton Street Bridge (Banana Bridge). The temporary footbridge used during the reconstruction of the Bedminster Bridge was re-erected permanently a few hundred metres up the Cut opposite St Luke's church (now demolished).

Vauxhall Bridge. Originally a pedestrian swing bridge to allow boats to sail along the Cut. Opened in 1900. Hydraulic power was supplied from the adjacent Underfall Yard. The bridge has been in fixed position since 1936.

And finally, the bridge that never was. **Narrow Quay/Canon's Marsh Road Bridge**. It was planned at a time when the car and concrete was king. In 1966, the City Council devised a development plan (see page 133) that included a proposal to fill in a section of the harbour and build a 'primary distributor road' running east/west over, and alongside, what remained of the docks.[5] The outcry was enormous and a rethink required.[6] Thankfully, by 1973, the docks were seen as a resource for recreation

Clifton Suspension Bridge was opened in 1864. Brunel's bridge was pronounced to be not only the strongest suspension bridge in the world but also the most beautiful.

and leisure rather than as an urban expressway for motor vehicles and the plan for this bridge was unceremoniously dumped.

Clifton Suspension Bridge. Bristol's iconic suspension bridge was spawned by a Bristol wine merchant, William Vick (d.1754), who left £1,000 for the erection of a bridge to span the highest point of the Avon Gorge – linking Clifton and Leigh Woods.[7]

The bequest generated a number of crazy submissions, the most sensible of which was I.K. Brunel's elegant, Egyptian styled suspension bridge. It was a project that Brunel was particularly fond of. 'My first child, my darling', he called it.[8] Work subsequently began in 1831 but was abandoned in 1853 when the money ran out. All hope of finishing the bridge appeared to be lost when a vital part of the structure, the cast-iron chains from which the deck was to be suspended, were put up for sale to recoup losses. The chains were subsequently purchased by the South Devon

Sparke Evans Park Footbridge (1902). Suspension bridge linking Sparke Evans Park to Paintworks, Bath Road.

Railway Company for use on their Saltash Bridge across the River Tamar. [9] For the next seven years two vast brick buttresses stood above the Avon Gorge like an abandoned gateway, a constant reminder of a thwarted dream.

And yet, a year after Brunel's death in 1860, construction resumed. Work began on a pared-down version of Brunel's original Egyptian vision – the sphinxes on the towers being a victim of cost-cutting. New chains were acquired from the short-lived Hungerford Bridge in London, another Brunel project, which had recently been demolished, in favour of a railway bridge.[10]

The Clifton Suspension Bridge was finally opened in 1864. Prior to opening, to test its strength, a 500-ton load of stone was spread evenly over the roadway and the footpaths.[11] Brunel's bridge was pronounced to be not only the strongest suspension bridge in the world but also the most beautiful.

Clifton Suspension Bridge in figures [12]
- **Height above high water:** 74.7m (245ft)
- **Total Span:** 214m (702ft)
- **Span between abutments:** 191m (627ft)
- **Height of pillars:** 22.3 m (73ft)
- **Weight:** 1,500 tons
- The securing chains are dug 21m (70ft) down into the rock.

Bristol's suspension bridges
- Clifton Suspension Bridge.
- Goal Ferry Bridge: links Wapping Wharf with Southville.
- Sparke Evans Park Bridge: links Sparke Evans Park to Paintworks, Bath Road.
- Castle Park Bridge: not over water, but crosses Lower Castle Street.

FERRIES

- The only way to cross the river -

Until the beginning of the 19th century Bristol had just one bridge across the Avon. Apart from Bristol Bridge the only way to cross the river was by ferry. Ferries were also used for the transport of animals. There is a painting (its present whereabouts is unknown) of Rownham Ferry (1820-22) by the Bristol artist Rolinda Sharples (1793-1838).

The picture shows a perilously crowded boat. Women in bonnets, men in top hats, children and babies are all packed together. Two lovers gaze into each other's eyes, while a couple of fellows study the latest news. Also on board is a frock-coated gentleman with his piebald horse!

Cumberland Basin, c.1850, with queue for Rownham Ferry (middle left).

Redcliffe Ferry, from Redcliffe Back to the Grove.
© Bristol Culture (Bristol Museum & Art Gallery).

Guinea Street Ferry, from Lower Guinea Street slipway to the Grove. © Bristol Culture (Bristol Museum & Art Gallery).

Broad Quay, An intriguing, if slightly wonky view of the quay. Note the use of geehoes for the transport of barrels. British School, c.1760. © Bristol Culture (Bristol Museum & Art Gallery).

- Ferries across the Avon and the Floating Harbour -

- **St Philips Ferry**. From Counterslip to St Philips. Replaced by a temporary wooden bridge in 1838; at that time it carried over 100,000 passengers a year.
- **Redcliffe Ferry**. From Redcliffe Backs to the Grove/Welsh Back. In 1875 the toll was a half penny. Replaced by Redcliffe Bascule Bridge, opened 1941.
- **Guinea Street Ferry**. From Lower Guinea Street slipway over to the Grove. Closed 1931.
- **Broad Quay to St Augustine's (The Butts)**. Replaced by the drawbridge.
- **Green Slip Ferry**. From Narrow Quay to Canon's Marsh.
- **Gas Works Ferry**. From Canon's Marsh Gas Works to Great Western Dock Yard.
- **Mardyke Ferry**. From Mardyke (Hotwells Road) to Chatham Wharf. Ceased to operate in 1967.

- **Rownham Ferry**. From Cumberland Slip to Somerset and, later, Clifton Bridge Railway Station. A difficult ferry to run because of the fast flowing water. At the very lowest tides, when the river was only several metres wide, a temporary bridge was erected. Ferry boats were anchored in the middle of the river, with planks connecting to slipways on either side. The more adventurous, or foolish, crossed on horseback. In 1610, two deaths were reported when this attempt at a short-cut went fatally wrong. One of those who died was John Snigge, who was intending to visit the Smythes at Ashton Court. His horribly decomposed remains were not found until six months later.[13] The Rownham Ferry closed in December 1932.

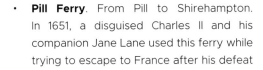

Rownham Ferry. A difficult ferry to run because of the fast flowing water. At the very lowest tides, when the river was only several metres wide, a temporary bridge was erected.

The Bristol Ferryboat Company was established in 1976 when the docks were no longer used for commercial trade.

- **Pill Ferry**. From Pill to Shirehampton. In 1651, a disguised Charles ll and his companion Jane Lane used this ferry while trying to escape to France after his defeat at the Battle of Worcester. A challenging ferry to operate due to the rapid ebb and flow of the river. Closed 1970.

- Ferries across the Avon New Cut -

- **Coronation Ferry/Gaol Ferry**. Linked Cumberland Road to St Paul's Church, Southville.

    First operated in 1838, boats were hauled by hand across the Cut with the use of a cable, or rowed. The cable could be lowered to allow boats to pass to and from the Bathurst Basin and beyond. At low tide planks would be placed on a boat in the middle of the water and pedestrians, as at Rownham Ferry, would walk across. They still had to pay a half-penny, though.

    Replaced by Gaol Ferry Bridge, which opened in October 1935.
- **Vauxhall Ferry**. From Cumberland Road to Vauxhall Yard. Closed with the opening of Vauxhall Bridge in 1900.

    Although these ferries are now long gone most of the slipways remain.[14]

- Twenty-first century ferries -

The Bristol Ferryboat Company was established in 1976 when the docks were no longer used for commercial trade. Initially, the Bristol Ferryboat Company offered leisure cruises around the harbour and up the Avon to the celebrated Beese's Tea Gardens and beyond to Hanham Lock. As well as themed boat trips timetabled services now plough the docks throughout the year.

In the 2010s, a rudimentary ferry, linking the S.S. Great Britain to Canon's Marsh – effectively the old Gas Works Ferry route – was introduced.

THE MAINTENANCE OF ROADS

- Tolls and turnpikes -

For many centuries there was uncertainty over who should be responsible for the upkeep of the roads. Should a householder be accountable for the patch in front of their house? Who should look after the busiest roads used by everyone?

Invariably, Bristol Corporation would wait until matters got really bad, or there was a special occasion, to undertake maintenance. Exceptional taxes would then have to be raised. The visit of royalty often spurred the Corporation into action. When Henry VII (1485-1509) visited in 1490 'the streets were newly paved'. It was a difficult balancing act. The city wanted to appear well managed, but not too prosperous, in case the King asked for extra benevolence. On this occasion Henry noted that the wives of the burgesses were 'sumptuously apparelled'.[15] The Corporation felt obliged to bequeath the King £500 as a mark of gratitude for his visit.

On occasions, benefactors would leave money with the express purpose of paving roads. In 1609, John Fownes left an annuity for raking and cleaning the walks in The Marsh (later to become Queen Square).[16] Dr Thomas White, in 1613, left money for the repair of roads, in particular ten miles of the road to Oxford, the whole of the road to Bath (via Hanham and Bitton), and five miles of all the main roads leading to Gloucester and Somerset.[17]

A street raker was appointed to keep the streets clear of horse dung and other offensive matter. Though following complaints of 'continued fouling of the streets' more funding was set aside in 1629 to tackle the problem.[18]

The problem of poorly maintained roads

Redcliffe Hill, 1820s. Who should look after the busiest streets?

leading to and from the city was eventually addressed with the establishment of the Bristol Turnpike Trust in 1727. Initially, four roads were turnpiked. The trust oversaw roads to Bedminster Down, Totterdown, Lower Easton and Kingswood (Don John's Cross).

Needless to say, there was widespread, and sometimes violent opposition. Tolls were an anathema to all that was English; they were an insult to freedom and liberty and an assault on the poor. The roads had always been free; this was authorised highway robbery. It was as if there was a tax on the air we breathed.

The Kingswood colliers asserted 'they would pay none of their taxes'. Turnpikes were chiefly intended to facilitate wheeled traffic. They were of little use to the colliers who mostly transported coal on horseback. A wrecking squad set out to destroy the newly erected gates and toll houses. Soldiers assisted at the gates to take the toll, but the next night, after they had withdrawn, the gates were cut down for a second time 'by person's disguised in women's apparel and high crowned hats'. [19] The Kingswood colliers did at least receive concessions, but every so often opposition flared. In 1749, men, this time shirtless, with their faces blacked, bored holes into the turnpike posts and blew them up with gunpowder.[20]

Several days of protest followed. The Ashton gate was demolished, followed by the pulling down of the Brislington and Whitchurch turnpikes. The trail of devastation was only halted when a posse of citizens and sailors, armed with cutlasses, arrested 27 of the protestors. Four were tried at the Taunton Assizes, two of whom were executed.[21]

More serious was the Bristol Bridge massacre of 1793. After 25 years the tolls on the rebuilt bridge were due to cease. But the Bridge Commissioners claimed they hadn't

Ashton Gate toll house, c.1820. Tolls were last collected here in 1866.

fully met their costs and duly re-imposed the toll. Demonstrations followed for several days. Eventually, the militia opened fire on the crowd, killing women, young men, old men and even a visitor from Castle Cary. The total number of fatal casualties was 14.[22] The Corporation realised its dreadful mistake and banned any enquiry on the grounds that Britain was at war with France and that such an inquest would provide an opportunity for agitators to destabilise the country.[23] Paradoxically, the demonstrators did not see themselves as revolutionaries, but as loyal Englishmen and women.

Although unpopular with the working person, turnpikes soon spread like a web across the whole country. The new un-rutted roads did at least allow for the development of a speedy coach service. It was on an August day in 1784 that the first Royal Mail coach, pulled by two horses, left the Rummer Tavern at 4.00pm. It reached Bath a couple of hours later. It then sped and bumped through the dark night, arriving at the London General Post Office by 8.00am. There was room for just four passengers. The charge for this exhilarating 16 hour, 10mph journey to the capital was

£1-8s-0d.[24]

For a less speedy and cheaper journey to London there were heavy old-style wagons. In 1809, a streamlined 'flying' wagon would leave Peter Street on Wednesday and arrive in London on Saturday. And for an even more leisurely pace there were slow wagons, some carrying a guard for passenger safety.[25]

By the early 19th century Bristol Turnpike Trust was the largest in the country. It was responsible for 180 miles of roads and had an excellent reputation for the maintenance of its highways.[26] Further improvements came in 1806, when an Act of Parliament made the Corporation responsible for the lighting, paving and cleansing of the streets.[27]

Tolls were finally abolished throughout the Bristol region in 1867, by which time there were no fewer than 15 toll gates scattered across the city.[28]

GEEHOES

- A very Bristol form of transport -

The wooden sledge is one of the simplest forms of transport. It is cheap to build and there's little that can go wrong. Sledges, or geehoes as they were known locally, were a very Bristolian form of transport. They were probably in use since the Bristol's earliest days – they are illustrated in a city charter dated 1347.

In 1615, the streets were in such a poor state it was decreed that no cart bound with iron wheels was allowed to come into the city – except to Broadmead and St Peter's pump.

When the traveller Celia Fiennes (1662-1741) visited Bristol in 1698 she noted the use of 'sleds to carry all things about'.[29] Thirty years earlier, Marmaduke Rawdon (1610-69), a merchant from York, made a similar observation. 'They use in the city most sleds to carry goods...' he wrote. He was less impressed, however, by the sledge drivers who were 'such rude people they will have their horses on a strangers back before they are aware'.[30]

Geehoes were effective for short journeys and were commonly used for the transport of barrels from the habourside. Up to three tuns (a tun contains 252 gallons) could be loaded onto a geehoe, which would then be pulled by two or three horses to nearby warehouses.

Daniel Defoe (1660-1731) was fascinated by them and noted that 'the pavements are worn smooth by them...in wet weather the streets are very slippery'.[31]

This primitive, yet effective form of transport, continued in use in Bristol until the 19th century.

© Bristol Culture (Bristol Museum & Art Gallery).

THE COLOSSUS OF ROADS

- John Loudon McAdam -

The Scottish engineer John Loudon McAdam (1756-1836) was appointed as general surveyor of Bristol Turnpike Trust in 1815.[32] At that time the roads in the district were all but impassable in bad weather and the Trust was on the verge of bankruptcy.[33]

Generally, there was no agreed method of road construction. Pot holes were filled with anything to hand – rocks, earth, clay, wood. In the long term such haphazard repairs only made road surfaces more perilous.

McAdam's 32 page booklet '*Remarks on the Present System of Road Making...*' was first published by J.M. Gutch of Small Street in 1816. The treatise was subsequently expanded and published in London.

McAdam's simple but effective proposal was to surface roads with stones no bigger than an inch in length. The layers of stones should be ten inches deep, and to allow for drainage, the centre of the road should be three inches higher than the side. With use, these stones would compact to form a smooth, dry(ish) surface. Tarmac (Tar Macadam), which uses heated tar to bind stones, is a later development of this idea.

Thanks to *macadamised* roads, road travel was soon to become bearable, not just in Bristol, but across the nation.

McAdam lived at a number of addresses in Bristol including, 32 Park Street and 23 then 29 Berkeley Square, Clifton. McAdam's son, James, succeeded him as surveyor of Bristol's roads and held the appointment until his death in 1857.[34]

Bicycles

This was written in 1909:
... it is only necessary to stand in one of the great arteries of Bristol at a time when factory and office work is ceasing for the dinner-hour, or for the day, to realise how great a factor in modern life the 'safety' bicycle has become.[35]

NINE O'CLOCK AND ALL IS WELL

- The introduction of the gas lamp -

Before the introduction of the gas lamp, when the sun set it was time to go to bed. There was no such thing as nightlife; the city was dark and apart from under the blanket activities, there was little else to do. Tallow candles gave out a weak smoky light and were expensive. Similarly, oil lamps were grimy and required trimming. Lunar phases were meticulously mapped; a clear night with a full moon was a night to be appreciated.

The curfew, announced by the ringing of St Nicholas's church bell, was called at 9.00pm. Anyone on the streets after that time was viewed with suspicion. Indeed it was a requirement to carry a lamp.

The first mention of street lighting in Bristol is in 1606 when lanterns were hung in significant places such as the gateways, the High Cross and the Quay.[36] In 1660, 530 of the principle householders were required in winter to hang a lantern containing a candle outside their house between 6.00pm and 9.00pm.[37]

Daniel Defoe commented that 'the city has long been lighted with lamps'.[38] This wasn't so in all the streets. In 1793, it was reported 'that in some of the more obscure streets the lamps are so scarce, that *the light in them is almost darkness*'.[39]

This was all to change with the introduction of gas lighting. Home produced coal gas was first used in 1811 by Mr John Breillat (1769 -1856), a silk dyer, to light his shop in Broadmead.[40] His trial was so successful that he put several lamps in the street outside. Thus Bristol can claim to be the first town in the country to

It was possible to walk the streets in relative safety. Gas lamps in High Kingsdown.

have a road lit (partially) by gas. Westminster Bridge in London was to follow the next year.

But gas lighting was slow to catch on. There was unease about Breillat having 'unholy dealings with an infernal power'. Besides, the gas smelt, it had to be stored in an unsightly gasometer and was generally viewed as dangerous. As one writer put it: 'The difference between inflammability and explosiveness was not fully appreciated'.[41]

Nevertheless, the Bristol Gas Company, with Breillat as manager, began operations in 1816. Soon a network of gas pipes connecting to a gasometer in Temple Back was dug under the city's roads.

The introduction of effective gas street lighting revolutionized people's lives. Although the light was yellow and smoky – the method of gas production had not yet been fully perfected – it was possible to walk the streets in relative safety. Every evening lamp-lighters would pace the streets wielding a long pole,

Bristol's first electricity generating station was at Temple Back. The supply commenced in 1893.[44]

with a burning wick attached, to light the gas lamps. At dawn they would return to switch off the lamps.

By 1858, Bristol's streets were lit by 3,150 gas lamps.[42] It took a while for gas to be used for purposes other than lighting. Cooking by gas didn't become common until the 1870s, when the Bristol Gas Company set up a scheme to rent cookers[43]. Gas fires were introduced ten years later.

ENDNOTES

1   *Arrowsmith's Dictionary of Bristol*, 1906, Arrowsmith, p.27-30.
2   Bettey, J.H., *The Landscape of Wessex*, 1980, Moonraker, p.104.
3   *Felix Farley's Bristol Journal*, 6 February 1747-8.
4   Latimer, J., *The Annals of Bristol – Nineteenth Century*, 1887, Bristol, p.342-3.
5   Bristol City Planning and Public Works Committee, *Bristol of the Future*, 1967, Bristol, p.25.
6   Priest, G. & Cobb, P., *The Fight for Bristol*, 1980, Bristol Civic Society and Redcliffe Press, p.13.
7   Buchanan, R.A & Williams, M., *Brunel's Bristol*, 1982, Redcliffe Press, p.15.
8   Rolt, L.T.C., *Isambard Kingdom Brunel*, 1989, Penguin, p.119.
9   Buchanan, R.A & Williams, M., op. cit., p.17.
10   Powell, R., *Brunel's Kingdom*, 1985, Watershed, p.58.
11   Andrews, A. & Pascoe, M., *Clifton Suspension Bridge*, 2008, Broadcast Books, p38.
12   ibid., p5.
13   Evans, J., *A Chronological Outline of the History of Bristol*, 1824, p.168.
14   Lord, J. & Southam, J., *The Floating Harbour*, 1983, Redcliffe Press, p.73-4.
15   Evans, J., op. cit., p.123.
16   ibid., p.167.
17   ibid., p.171.
18   Evans, J., op. cit., p.176.
19   Seyer, S., *Memoirs Historical and Topographical of Bristol*, 1823, Bristol, p.575.
20   Poole, S. & Rogers, N., *Bristol from Below, 2017*, The Boydell Press, p.172.
21   Seyer, S., *Memoirs Historical and Topographical of Bristol*, 1823, Bristol, p.594-5.
22   Manson, M., *Riot! The Bristol Bridge Massacre of 1793*, 1997, Past & Present Press, p.75.
23   ibid., p.89.
24   Tombs, R.C., *The Bristol Post*, 1899?, Arrowsmith, p.20.
25   Shiercliffe, E., *The Bristol and Hotwell Guide*, 1809, p.155.
26   Bettey, J. H. *The Landscape of Wessex*, 1980, Moonraker, p.138.
27   Ralph, E., *The Streets of Bristol*, 2001(Reprint), Bristol Branch of the Historical Association, p.12.
28   Latimer, J. *Annals of Nineteenth Century Bristol*, 1897, W. & F. Morgan. p.428.
29   Bettey, J.H., op. cit., p.60.
30   ibid., p.52.
31   ibid., p.62.
32   Hutton, S., *Bristol and its Famous Associations*, 1907, Arrowsmith, p.397.
33   Latimer, J., op. cit., p.64.
34   Tombs, R.C., op. cit., p.36.
35   Stone, G.F., *Bristol As It Was and As It Is*, 1909, Walter Reid, p.220.
36   Ralph, E., *The Streets of Bristol*, 2001 (Reprint), Bristol Branch of the Historical Association, p.16
37   ibid., p.16.
38   ibid., p.17.
39   Matthews, W., *A New History of Bristol or Complete Guide*, 1794, (Facsimile edition) p.50.
40   Latimer, J. *Annals of Nineteenth Century Bristol*, 1897, W. & F. Morgan. p.43.
41   Stone, G.F., op. cit., p.278.
42   ibid., p.1.
43   ibid., p.278.
44   ibid., p.279.

POWER TO THE PRINTERS

- Bristol's first newspaper -

Printers and publishers are powerful people. They can control a medium that supports the status quo; likewise, they can propagate anti-establishment views. Until the repeal of the Printing Act in 1663, there were strict regulations on the press. Although Caxton first established his printing press in 1476, it wasn't until more than 200 years later, in 1702, that Bristol had its first newspaper, *The Bristol Post Boy*. The *Bristol Post Boy* is regarded as the first provincial newspaper to be published in England.[1]

In 1712, a newspaper tax – some called it a tax on knowledge – was introduced. Even so, during the span of 18th century at least 25 different locally produced weekly news sheets were published in Bristol.[2] Among the many titles – *Bristol Journal, Bristol Mercury, Bristol Weekly Intelligencer, Bristol Advertiser* – one name stands out: Farley. Three generations of the Farley family oversaw a number of newspapers. Wives, sons, daughters and nieces were all involved. There was *Felix Farley's Bristol Journal; Sam Farley's Bristol*

It wasn't until 1858 that Bristol had its own daily paper, the *Western Daily Press*. In 1886 the *Western Daily Press* moved to a custom-designed building in Baldwin Street.

Newspaper and *Sarah Farley's Bristol Journal*. Samuel Farley also published newspapers in Exeter and Salisbury.[3]

Elizabeth Farley (1710-79), who took over the running of *Felix Farley's Bristol Journal* when her husband died in 1753, has the distinction of being the first newspaper

Bristol Times and Mirror office, built 1902-4, St Stephen's Street. The Bristol Times and Mirror first rolled off the presses in 1865. It was incorporated into the Western Daily Press in 1932.

proprietor to be prosecuted for libel after publishing a series of articles on Whig corruption. She was found not guilty.[4]

Even so, before the days of investigative journalism, the coverage of local news was minimal. The newspapers – one large sheet, printed double-sided and folded – mainly contained small advertisements, details of newly arrived and departing ships, court reports, the latest debates from Parliament and syndicated articles from London and abroad. The typography was dense, there were no shouting headlines. These weekly papers were shared and read in coffee houses and inns. They made Bristolians feel connected with the outside world. As Dr Samuel Johnson (1709-84) said: 'Knowledge is diffused among our people by the news-papers'.[5]

The newspaper tax was abolished in 1855. Soon after, in 1858, Bristol had its own daily paper, the Western Daily Press. Even though newspapers only sold for a penny per copy, there was good money to be made from advertising. In 1886, the Western Daily Press moved to a custom-designed building in Baldwin Street. The print machines were in an airy room on the top floor, while instant communication between staff was enabled throughout the building by speaking tubes.

Provincial newspapers were doing well until the 1920s, when press baron, Lord Rothermere (1868-1940), plotted to grab a wadge of the local action. His London papers, the Daily Mirror and the Daily Mail, were delivered to Bristol by the early morning train. Along with his Bristol Evening World, these cheap and engaging tabloids gave the Bristol press a run for its money. In response, a group of local business people and civic leaders established a new and truly Bristol paper. Reconditioned presses were set up in an old leather warehouse in Silver Street. And so the Evening Post – mast header The Paper you have so eagerly awaited – first hit the streets in 1932.[6]

For many years the Evening Post and the Western Daily Press were seen as the heart of the community; newspapers that Bristol could be proud of. But by the 1950s the glory days of print journalism were starting to wane. In 1960, Bristol United Press, the owner of the Bristol Evening Post acquired the ailing Western Daily Press for a mere £250.[7]

From the 1950s newspapers faced a rival for news dissemination. BBC TV's South and West Region was Bristol-based, while the independent television channel Television Wales and the West (TWW) (1958) had offices in Cardiff, London and Bristol. TWW was replaced in 1967 by Harlech TV (HTV), with studios on the Bath Road. Harlech TV, named after the head of the company, Lord Harlech (1918-85), was backed by the celebrity glamour couple Richard Burton (1926-84) and Elizabeth Taylor (1932-2011) alongside ex-Goon, Harry Secombe (1921-2001).

In 1974, in a valiant show of confidence, the Western Daily Press and the Evening Post moved from Silver Street into a modernist office on Temple Way. A feature of this distinctive building was its glass fronted print hall where the papers – there were several daily editions – could be seen rolling off the presses. For a while the presses were busy. Rival newspaper, the *Bath Chronicle* was printed here, as were the local *Observer* free-sheets.

The demise of print journalism was slow, but new technology wrought unstoppable change. The once strong print unions – in the 1960s you couldn't get a print job unless you were a union member– were able to do little to protect their workforce.

From 2009, the printing of Bristol United Press's papers, then owned by the *Daily Mail* and General Trust Group, was moved to Didcot, Oxfordshire.[8] The impressive press-hall stood silent until it was demolished. A 12-storey block for student accommodation, the *Print Hall,* now stands on its former footprint. From 2012 the *Evening Post,* no longer an evening paper, was renamed *The Bristol Post.*

Print journalism continues to face grave challenges from 24-hour internet news. Yet, serious fact-finding journalism remains an essential part of the democratic process. This is as true regionally as it is nationally. Alongside

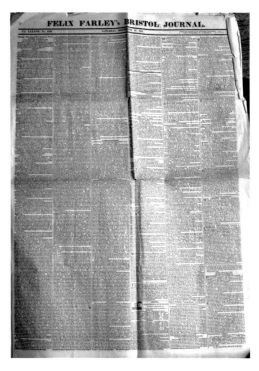

Felix Farley's Bristol Journal. The typography was dense, there were no shouting headlines.

The Bristol Post, independent media such as *Bristol 24/7* and *Bristol Cable* continue to carry out important investigative work. We lose our local newspapers and journalists at our peril.

- Bristol Channel -

The first breakfast-time TV programme

In the early days of television some areas of Bristol experienced poor television reception due to the city's hilly topography. Consequently, in 1972, Rediffusion set up a community television service, *Bristol Channel.* Rather than broadcast through the airwaves *Bristol Channel's* novel approach was to transmit programmes directly into viewer's homes via a cable. From a tiny studio in Broad Plain this low budget TV station planned to offer 15 hours a week of news, sport and drama. *Bristol Channel* introduced the first breakfast-time TV programmes shown in the UK.

This pioneering venture was short lived. *Bristol Channel* closed in 1975 due to Government restrictions on programming and a viewing audience too small to be viable.[9]

THE COMMUNICATIONS REVOLUTION
- Telegrams, telephones and post boxes -

The electric telegraph was initially used to send messages in Morse code to railway signalmen.

However, in 1851, the Midland Railway company opened its telegraph system for wider access. At this early stage the telegraph's potential was under appreciated and was mostly used for the transmission of horse racing results.[10]

In the following year the Great Western Railway established telegraph lines that ran from London to Exeter via Bristol. This time the telegraph was utilized for the more sober purpose of transmitting brief summaries of Parliamentary debate to the local press.

It didn't take long for journalists and newspapers to realise that news could be transferred almost instantly. Indeed, the power of this new method of communication was such that by 1870 the Post Office offered an interconnected nationwide telegram service.

Telegrams in Bristol were delivered swiftly by uniformed telegraph messenger boys. In the 1890s there were over 160 messenger boys employed by the Bristol Post Office.[11] Many of these lads were only 13 or 14 years old and recruited straight from school.

Telegrams were, however, expensive. At a rate of one shilling for 20 words they were chiefly used for emergencies and matters of life and death.[12]

The telegraph was soon augmented by Alexander Grahame Bell's telephone. Bell addressed a *Scientific Soiree* at the Bristol Museum in 1877 where, to great applause, he showed the audience a telephone and

In 1898, an extensive new telephone exchange was built off Baldwin Street in the eponymous Telephone Avenue.

The first Penny Post Office, next to the Exchange in Corn Street, was established in 1793.

explained its construction. Bell proclaimed 'that it might seem a startling fact that one person might converse with his friend by word of mouth though separated by hundreds of miles of space'. He said he would do his best to 'explain how the seeming impossibility was made feasible'.[13]

Two years later, the Western Counties and South West Wales Telephone Company set up business in Bristol. At first, not surprisingly, the number of subscribers was limited. The hitch being, you could only phone somebody who also had a phone! In the first three months only 20 subscribers joined.[14] Telephone use was almost entirely for business purposes – for personal communication the penny post was still the preferred method of contact.

By 1887, telephone lines from Bristol were connected to Cardiff, Swansea and Gloucester. There was a fixed annual charge of £60 for calls to South Wales and £30 to Gloucester. In 1892, the local telephone service was absorbed into the National Telephone Company. In 1879, there had been just 25 customers; by 1901 the number had increased to 15,000.

In 1898 an extensive new telephone exchange was built off Baldwin Street in the eponymous Telephone Avenue. At the start of the 20th century the annual number of locally made calls exceeded seven million. The age of the telephone had arrived.

Penny Post

The first Penny Post Office, next to the Exchange in Corn Street, was established in 1793. The opening hours were long: letters could be taken to the Post Office between 7.00am and 9.00pm. There were then three deliveries each day – at 9am, noon and 6.00pm – to all parts of the city, including Clifton and the Hotwell.[15]

The distinctive red pillar box was introduced into Bristol in the mid-1850s. Initially, there were concerns about the safety of early designs. Nimble fingered street urchins would willingly demonstrate how they could reach into a letter box and

The distinctive red pillar box was introduced into Bristol in the mid-1850s. This one, in Henleaze, is a collector's item. It is one of the few pillar boxes in England from the 11 month reign of Edward VIII.

retrieve correspondence.[16]

Nevertheless, by 1879, letter boxes were cleared by postmen at least four times a day. By today's standards the excellence of the Victorian postal service is barely imaginable. A letter posted in Bristol at 2.10pm would be delivered anywhere in London on the same day.[17] By the end of the 19th century there were over 350 pillar and wall letter boxes scattered across the city.[18]

ENDNOTES

1   Anon, *Early Bristol Newspapers*, 1956, Corporation of Bristol, p.5.
2   ibid., p.32.
3   ibid., p.5-20.
4   Duffus, J., *The Women who Built Bristol*, 2018, Tangent, p.164.
5   Porter, R., *English Society in the Eighteenth Century*, 1990, Penguin Books, p.234.
6   Penney, J., *All The News That's Fit To Print*, 2001, Bristol Branch of the Historical Association, p.27-8.
7   ibid., p.33.
8   https://en.wikipedia.org/wiki/Bristol_Post Accessed 03/05/2020
9   http://www.rediffusion.info/Bristol/ Accessed 03/05/2020.

10   Latimer, J., *The Annals of Bristol – Nineteenth Century*, 1887, Bristol, p.325.
11   ibid., p.223.
12   British Telecom only discontinued the telegram service in 1982.
13   *Bristol Times and Mirror*, 18 October 1877.
14   Stone, G.F., *Bristol As It Was and As It Is*, 1909, Walter Reid, p.277.
15   Shiercliffe, E., *The Bristol and Hotwell Guide*, 1809, p.152.
16   *Bristol Mercury*, 23 February 1856. Thank you Eugene Byrne for this information.
17   Hall Ellis, M.J., *The Early Years of the Telephone Service in Bristol 1879-1931*, 1985?, British Telecommunications Ltd, p.1.
18   Tombs, R.C., *The Bristol Post*, 1899?, Arrowsmith, p.137.

EARTH, WIND, AIR AND FLOOD

THE AIR WE BREATHE

- Weather -

Bristolians have always taken a keen interest in the weather. Of course, in the days of sail the weather was an important influence on the coming and going of ships. In the Commercial Rooms (now a J.D. Wetherspoon's pub) in Corn Street, there was, and still is, a large dial on the wall indicating the wind direction which would be watched keenly by the city's merchants as they ate their roast beef and Yorkshire pudding. In City Hall, as a nod to past times, there is a wind indicator on the clock in the entrance hall.

The region's weather has been described as 'basically, mild, damp and dull compared with other areas of Britain'. This is due to maritime influences which are carried up the Severn Estuary and along the Bristol Channel. Snow is exceptional, falling on an average of five days a year and it rarely settles – or 'pitches' as Bristolians say – for long.

Bristol weather chronicler Barry Horton explains 'City weather is always warmer than the countryside because concrete takes a long time to warm up and cool down, creating a 'heat island' effect.'[1]

Back in the 18th century Bristol's mild climate was used as draw for visitors to the Hot Well. In 1793 William Matthews, in his *Bristol Guide,* noted that:

Bristol... stands in a most delightful and healthy Country, and is surrounded with numerous verdant hills, some of moderate, others of towering height, particularly to the north, which defend it from the cold winds and render its situation very warm and comfortable.[2]

Matthews went on to say that Bristol's air:

...is well known and experienced to be undeniably and notably salubrious. Its soil is dry; and the damps of some moist countries and atmospheres are here unknown.[3]

Indeed, Bristol's climate was so salubrious Matthews warned:

Some invalids of Bristol whom business or curiosity have led to London, have soon found themselves worse than before, and (been) obliged to make a hasty retreat to their native air.

Snow is exceptional. It rarely settles – or 'pitches' as Bristolians say – for long.

The air quality for those living and working near the docks was further degraded with the building of the floating harbour. By 1815, even Matthews was warning that:

'...in the summer season particularly, the water acquires a dark unpleasant surface; and where it is most subject to the reception of drains emits a rather offensive smell.'

It wasn't just the emissions from factories and workshops that polluted the atmosphere. Until the 1950s local coal was used for nearly all domestic heating. A constant stench of coal fires hung in the air and clung to buildings. One has only to look at old photographs of Bristol to see how the city was blackened by smoke. Even on sunny days visibility was poor.

Despite all this, at the beginning of the 20th century Bristol's air was certainly cleaner than London's.

'The Climate of Bristol is mild and the hygrometric state of the atmosphere is generally high; in winter it is rarely subject to extreme colds, or in summer to extreme heats. The air in the lower parts of the city is soft and relaxing rather than bracing; but, as the city lies on so many different levels and so many soils, no general description will apply to the whole....

'The air on the higher levels is very pure and bracing, and readily shows the presence of ozone on the application of the proper test. It is exceedingly well adapted for the invalid, who can here choose the climate most suitable to their constitutions. Those who require a soft mild atmosphere have for their selection the lower and sheltered slopes, and those who require highly ionised and bracing air, fresh from the Bristol Channel can get all they desire on Clifton, Durdham Down and Redland.'

Dictionary of Bristol, Arrowsmith, 1906 [7]

But Matthews wasn't giving the whole picture with regard to the purity of the air. In 1739, the poet Alexander Pope (1677-1744) commented that his first impression of Bristol was of 'twenty odd pyramids smoking over the town'[4]. These tall brick cones, many over 60 feet high, were used for the production of pottery and glass. The smoke from these industries, along with fumes from the sugar boilers, soap makers, tallow chandlers, foundries and many other industries, meant that Bristol's air was far from wholesome. When the dilettante Horace Walpole (1717-97) visited in 1766 he said the city was 'the dirtiest great shop I ever saw'.[5] The editors of Daniel Defoe's *A tour through the island of Great Britain* (1779) wrote: 'on account of the trades that require large fires...there is generally a thick cloud of smoke over the city'.[6]

It is no coincidence that the wealthier classes preferred to live in Clifton, on the western side of the city, where they could breathe the untainted air from the prevailing westerly winds.

It is worth noting the *Dictionary of Bristol* didn't mention the air pollution to the east of the city. A report of 1895 on the air quality at Crew's Hole, the centre of Bristol's chemicals industries, made alarming reading. Here, 20 chimneys poured out a noxious cocktail of acid-rain-forming vapours from the tar, alkali, ammonia and brick works.

Nationally, the turning point for air pollution was the great London smog of December 1952. The smog, a mix of smoke and fog, brought the capital to a halt for four days. It was so dense you could not see across the road. Smog was not just a nuisance, it was deadly. It is estimated that over 4,000 people died of respiratory disease directly related to this pollution. Following this, the Clean Air Act (1956) was introduced. The Clean Air Act prohibited 'dark smoke' from chimneys and did much to improve air quality. The increasing use of oil and natural gas in the 1960s also enabled a switch to cleaner fuel.

Today air pollution is more insidious. We may have stopped soot and sulphur dioxide belching out of chimneys but with an estimated 500,000 car movements in and out of the city every day, it is carbon omissions that we need to tackle. Five people die each week in Bristol as a result of high levels of air pollution, a study in 2019 revealed.[8]

The City Council checks air quality and has automatic monitoring stations around the city. Even so areas of Bristol regularly break World Health pollution guidelines. Air pollution is still regarded as a top public health threat. City centre changes to traffic routes planned to be introduced in 2022 to meet Clean Air Zone compliance is arguably a sticking plaster solution.

Watching the weather and monitoring air quality is as important as ever as we gauge the long-term damage we are doing to our planet.

2009-2010. The coldest winter for 27 years. Sledging in St Andrew's Park.

- Bristol Weather Extremes -

Highest temperature

2000-2018	33C August 2003
1900-2000	35C August 1995

Lowest temperature

2000-2018	-9C December 2010
1900-2000	-10C January 1982

Wettest month

2000-2018	271mm November 2009
1900-2000	258mm September 1918

Snowiest year

2000-2018	2009/10
1900-2000	1962/3

Windiest day

2000-2018	Jan 2007 gust to 68mph
1900-2000	Jan 1990 gust to 91mph
2022	18 February gust up to 55mph.

Thanks to Barry Horton, 'The Bristol Weatherman'.

SMELLY OLD TOWN

- The stink of the city -

O f all the senses, smell is the most neglected. Some smells stick in the throat and leave a gritty taste in the mouth; acid smells clear the nasal passages and make the eyes water. Other smells reek of nostalgia – comforting, jolting us back to childhood and less complicated times. Before smoking was banned in public places in 2007 you could smell a pub a mile off. A few smells are so pervasive that you crave a shower and a change of clothes.

Courage's brewery filled Victoria Street with a hoppy, malty smell.

Even today, if you close your eyes and walk around Bristol it is not difficult to identify your location by smell. Natural smells include the comforting odour of cut grass on the Downs while, in the height of summer, the lime trees that line so many roads exude an intoxicating perfume. And in the Spring, the smell of the wild garlic which coats the shady woodland floor of the Frome Valley or Leigh Woods is unmistakable.

A not unfamiliar smell in Bristol is of roasting coffee. The aroma of coffee from Brian Wogan's hangs over the gateway to Bristol at the end of the M32. In the past, Carwardine's coffee shop, at the top of Park Street, roasted beans so violently that billowing clouds of smoke could be hazardous to traffic. Then there are the warm fragrances, evocative of exotic shores, percolating from Bart Spices on York Road. And dare I say it, the earthy herbal whiff of illicit skunk marijuana is not an altogether alien feature of the bohemian streets of Montpelier.

Going back a few years, Courage's – formerly George's – brewery (now Finzel's

Reach), filled the Victoria Street air with a hoppy, malty smell. While in Bedminster the gentle tang of tobacco from Wills's various manufactories infused the nearby streets. In the middle of the 20th century the whiff from the faggot and pea shop on Redcliffe Hill made many mouths water.

Mostly, though, smells are unwelcome. In the past, the worst stink came from the Frome and the Avon, which acted as depositories for raw sewage. Before their tidal flow was interrupted by the building of the Floating Harbour in 1809 these rivers had at least benefited from a twice daily cleanse. But once this natural flushing process was interrupted, during the warmer months, a foul miasma would hang over the near-stagnant docks.

In 1825 it was reported that the pong emitted from the Frome was 'disgusting to the smell and nauseous to the stomach'.[9] It was an ongoing problem. After a particularly hot summer a writ was issued against the Dock Company ordering it to make whatever alterations were necessary to clear the floating

In the 19th and early 20th century a pleasing chocolaty aroma hung like a haze over Union Street in central Bristol.

harbour of sewage.[10] Eventually, in 1832, a young Isambard Kingdom Brunel was brought in to advise on the difficulty. The solution was to build an 'underfall' which enabled the flow of a cleansing current through the floating harbour.

Until the introduction of odourless natural gas from the North Sea in the 1970s, gasworks were notoriously foul-smelling. The staff of Bristol Cathedral seriously regretted the sale of the western corner of Canon's Marsh in the 1820s for the building of a gas works. Initially gas was made from whale oil. But when the process changed in the 1840s, whereby gas was produced by heating coal, a most disagreeable sulphurous pall hung over the area.[11]

For many years, on a still summer's day, the lingering stink of sweet decay from the huge piles of bones waiting to be processed at Cole's bone yard – also known as the Glue Factory – on the Feeder Road could be smelled from miles away.

The stinkometer went off the scale in 1885 when a whale that had been beached at Littleton on Severn on 15 January was brought to Cole's. After being viewed by thousands of inquisitive spectators, the unfortunate mammal was rendered down into fat and fertilizer (bone meal).[12]

Bone processing on the Feeder Road site ceased in the 1980s. Elsewhere, a slightly urinous odour lingers around the west end of Coronation Road, Southville, where Bristol's last tannery owned by Thomas Ware and Sons (operating since 1840), continue to produce high quality leather.

Fry's Sweet Success

In the 19th and early 20th century a pleasing chocolaty aroma hung like a haze over Union Street in central Bristol.

Dr Joseph Storrs Fry (1728-87), a Quaker businessman, first sold cocoa in the mid-18th century from his small shop in Narrow Wine Street.[13] Then, cocoa, which came from South America and the Caribbean, was a bitter drink mostly consumed for its supposed health giving properties.[14]

The nature of cocoa consumption changed forever in 1847 when Fry's made Britain's first eating chocolate bar. Production increased as new merchandise was introduced and sold worldwide. *Fry's Chocolate Cream* and, later, *Fry's Turkish Delight* became household names. In 1902, milk chocolate was launched in the form of the *Five Boys* chocolate bar. The enigmatic, and slightly disturbing, *Five Boys* featured on the wrapper a boy's face who's expression morphed from desperation to joy, when he realises 'Its Fry's'.

By 1914 Fry's was one of Bristol's foremost companies, employing over 5,000 people.[15] In 1917 Fry's merged with chocolate rivals, Cadbury's.

The Fry and Cadbury families were Quakers. The work day started with a short service – a couple of hymns and a prayer. It was hard graft: 'We daren't talk and we daren't laugh' wrote Bertha Milton, a so-called Fry's Angel. But at least it was a regular income.[16]

The company built a new factory at Keynsham. The model factory, Somerdale, which opened in 1935, was set in green fields with its own railway siding.

The last Fry family member connected with the business was Cecil Fry, who died in 1952.[17] The Somerdale site closed in 2011 with a loss of 400 jobs. Cadbury's is now owned by Kraft Foods and its chocolate is made in Poland.

Fry's model factory, Somerdale, opened 1935, was set in green fields with its own railway siding.

H.J Packer and Co established the first chocolate factory in Greenbank in 1903.

Elizabeth Shaw

In Greenbank, a chocolatety fragrance from the Elizabeth Shaw factory (closed 2006) pervaded the neighbourhood. H.J Packer and Co established the first chocolate factory in Greenbank in 1903. Over the years there have been a number of owners. Products made at Greenbank included *Famous Names Liqueur Chocolates*, *Walnut Whirls*, *Mint Crisps* and *After Dinner Mints*.

VIOLENT TEMPESTS

- Floods and flood defences -

Being at the confluence of the River Frome and the tidal Avon Bristol has always been at the mercy of the weather and the tide.

The earliest record of local flooding occurs in 1258 when there was a 'prodigious inundation' as 'a violent tempest of rain fell on the waters of the Severn from Shrewsbury towards Bristol, as has not been seen in our days...By this flood some men were destroyed, many children and innumerable animals of various kinds (were killed).'[18]

The city received a direct hit in October 1483 when according to *Ricart's Calendar* 'The greatest flood and the greatest wind at Bristol and in the country thereabouts that ever was seen... Great damage was done at Bristol in the merchant's houses and cellars in wool and salt.' Two ships were lost and many boats waiting to sail up to the docks were damaged.

In 1606, a natural phenomenon occurred not usually associated with this part of the world. Without warning, on Tuesday 20 January, a wall of water swept up the Bristol Channel breaking the banks of the river and causing the death of livestock and over 2,000 people.[19] By the time the wave reached North Somerset it is estimated to have been 25ft high. In Kingston Seymour, a plaque in the church porch records the calamity:

'An inundation of the sea water by overflowing and breaking down the Sea banks; happened in this Parish of Kingstone-Seamore, and many others adjoining; by reason whereof many Persons were drown'd and much Cattle and Goods, were lost: the water in the Church was five feet high...'

This flood has puzzled experts. The weather was fine and prior to the inundation the sea was sucked back. Some say geological evidence points to a *tsunami*, others that it was storm surge caused by a lethal mix of high tide, low pressure and strong winds from the south west.

In 1606, a wall of water swept up the Bristol Channel breaking the banks of the river and causing the death of livestock and over 2,000 people.

In Kingston Seymour, North Somerset, a plaque records the 1606 flood.

By the late 19th century, flooding occurred in the new suburbs with increasing regularity. Stapleton Road: the Black Swan is in the middle distance. © Bristol Culture (Bristol Museum & Art Gallery).

In 1672 'meadows about the city were overflowed four feet and a half upright; it drowned an abundance of cattle, carried away a great deal of hay and did much damage to the corn'.[20] A high tide in 1687 'did great damage to the merchant's cellars; a boat came up to the entrance of Baldwin Street; and in the country it drowned many cattle'.[21] 1703 was a particularly bad year. On mid-summers day 'a very great storm of hail and rain fell in this city, while in November a tempest swept across the country. In Bristol, three pinnacles from St Stephen's church were blown down and lead from the roof of St Philip's was 'wrapped up like a piece of folded cloth'. A conjunction of a high tide and rain water coming down the Avon and Frome exacerbated the difficulties. Half the city was flooded. 'A boat might have sailed through the whole of Temple Street', while parts of Baldwin Street were under two foot of water.[22]

Over the years, as Bristol expanded, the natural drainage system of the land was put under increasing pressure. Unscrupulous developers built houses on flood plains and soggy land alongside brooks. As a result, by the late 19th century, flooding occurred in the new Victorian suburbs with increasing regularity. On 22-23 October 1882, the Frome and its tributaries flooded Ashley Road, Sevier Street, Mina Road, Stapleton Road and Pennywell Road. Houses in Baptist Mills were so badly damaged that they had to be demolished.

Flood marker for the 1882 flood, Mina Road, St Werburgh's.

After 48 hours of rain on the 8-9 March 1889, 150 acres on the banks of the Frome were submerged. In Broadmead, the water was nearly five feet high. Bridewell Police Station, middle distance, from Nelson Street. **Picture by Earnest A Parkman.** © Bristol Culture (Bristol Museum & Art Gallery).

After 48 hours of rain on 8-9 March 1889, 150 acres on the banks of the Frome were yet again submerged. In Broadmead, the water was nearly five feet high. Cheltenham Road and a greater part of Bedminster were likewise flooded.

Much of St Philip's was below the high tide mark.[23] The name St Philip's Marsh is a bit of a giveaway. On 12 February 1899 the Avon flooded many streets in St Philip's Marsh. To make matters worse the Malago Brook overflowed in Bedminster while further downstream Rownham Railway Station was under several feet of water.

The culverting of brooks and the straightening of the Frome, including the removal of several old mills and their adjoining dams,[24] during the first half the 20th century, went some way to solving these problems.[25]

Yet flooding continued. The Zetland Road junction with the Cheltenham Road was another flooding hot-spot. Here, water from the Cranbrook would spill out onto the surrounding streets. The Cheltenham Road flooding was alleviated to a certain degree by a relief culvert which was operational by 1902. But inundations still occurred in 1920 and 1922 when the Cranbrook, yet again, caused floods of at least a foot deep at the Zetland Road junction.

After World War Two, further ambitious projects were initiated. Today, few people are aware of the network of tunnels that run under central Bristol. To the north of the city, between 1951 and 1961, a seven mile long storm water sewer was built which empties into the Avon Gorge.

The 'great flood' of 1968 put Bristol's

In 1920 and 1922, the Cranbrook caused floods of at least a foot deep at the Cheltenham Road junction with Zetland Road.

storm defences to the test when nearly seven inches of rain fell on the Mendips in six and a half hours. A wall of water swept down the Chew Valley causing widespread damage in Pensford and Keynsham. At Pensford the A37 road bridge was washed away. Seven people died. In the worst single incident three people were drowned when their car was swept off Bath Hill Bridge at Keynsham. Water also came storming down the Dundry and Withywood slopes. Vans and lorries were swept away, Symes Avenue, Hartcliffe, was flooded and Marksbury Road, Bedminster, was left under several feet of water.[26] The Wills cigarette factory in East Street, Bedminster, was flooded to a depth of five feet. A few days later a near riot broke out when millions of 'flood damaged cigarettes' were dumped on the Corporation tip at Lawrence Weston and swiftly scavenged.

During the clean-up operation in Keynsham Prince Philip, the Duke of Edinburgh, flew in by helicopter to offer so-called moral support. But his visit was so desultory few people recognised him.

It was clear that Bristol's flood defences needed further strengthening. The Malago Storm Water Interceptor, which empties into the Cut just opposite the Old Gaol, was built between 1971 and 1974. This was followed by the construction of another two massive storm drains under the city. The Northern Foul Water Interceptor, started in 1992, runs under Lawrence Hill, the M32 and then heads in a westerly direction deep under Cotham and Clifton. At its widest the tunnel is 10.62 metres in diameter, big enough to drive a bus through.

The 'great flood' of 1968 put Bristol's storm defences to the test. East Street, Bedminster, the morning after. The man in the crash helmet is riding on a shop counter. © Bristol Post.

It was clear that Bristol's flood defences needed further strengthening. Duckmoor Road, Ashton, 10 July 1968.

In 1994 Wessex Water offered the public the novel experience of a walk under the Frome and the M32 before the flood gates were opened.[27]

The final piece of the jigsaw was the completion in 2009, using drill and blast techniques, of a £9 million tunnel 75 metres below the surface running from Frogmore Street to Woodland Road in Clifton. From there it connects to the Northern Foul Water Interceptor.

To the north of Bristol, those attractive rush-fringed ponds at Abbey Wood, Aztec West, Bradley Stoke and Cribbs Causeway are not merely a landscape architect's conceit, but a requirement of planning permission. These ponds act as water detention reservoirs holding back millions of gallons of surface rain water from car parks, roofs and roads that would otherwise flood the River Frome catchment area.

Developments over the last hundred years have considerably decreased the risk of flooding.

Looking to the future, maybe the threat of a tidal surge will be reduced with the erection of the much debated Severn Barrage, while at the same time generating electricity?

Tides

A feature of the port of Bristol has always been its challenging tidal range. The Severn Estuary acts like a funnel and has a significant effect on the tides. At Avonmouth, in the Spring, the difference between the height of the water at low and high tide can be an astounding 13-14 m. This is the second largest tidal range in the World, exceeded only by Bay of Fundy in Canada at 15.5 m.

High tide at the Cumberland Basin is 10 minutes later than that at Avonmouth.

HEAVY WEATHER

- Excerpts from Adams's Chronicle of Bristol [28] -

Adams's Chronicle contains an annual list of magistrates and a brief idiosyncratic account of what happened each year. It covers the period 1216-1639.

1483 15 October, 'a wonderful great flood in most part of the land from Bristol to the Mount ...Great damage was done at Bristol in the merchant's houses and cellars in wool and salt'. To make matters worse, the chronicler notes, the moon was eclipsed 'between two and three hours' ... 'giving but little light.' But then 'waxed clear again.' Two thousand men, women and children are said to have drowned.

1483 'The greatest flood and the greatest wind at Bristol and in the country thereabouts that ever was seen.'

1517 'This year it continued to rain from Whitsuntide to Michelmas.'

1544 'A marvellous great thunder lasting from eight o'clock at night until four in the morning.' One man killed by lightning.

1559 'At Candlemas there arose so great a storm of wind and rain that did much hurt in diverse places.'

1564 '21 December to 3 January there was such a hard frost, that the Thames of London was so hard frozen that men, women and children went upon it... At Bristol and Hungroad it was so hard frozen that people passed over the channel upon ice...'

1604 'On 4 October was the greatest snow that was ever known by the memory of man, which continued four days. And by reason that the leaves were on the trees, very many were thrown down by the roots, and the limbs of many others were broken in pieces.'

1607 'About All-hallow-tide' (end of October) 'began a frost, which continued until February following. In which time Severn and Wye were so hard frozen that trowes and boats could not come down for ice... Yet all this time the Back and the Quay and so downwards to Hungroad was not frozen as reported in *anno* 1564.'

1610 'This winter proved very foul and stormy which caused much shipwreck in sundry places...'

1623 'This winter fell out extreme cold and frosty, with such store of snow that many fowl and cattle died for want of sustenance: which cold lasted until May; and the summer after that proved very dry; grass and hay was scant, and water failed in many places whereby cattle were liken to starve again in many places.'

1634 A great wind whipped the snow into drifts which eventually formed ice. '...people were forced to break it up with pickaxes, bars of iron and hatchet, being so thick and hard like unto great stones digged out of rocks...all our hauliers and carters were hired and compelled many days to carry it and throw it into the river.'

THE COLDEST WINTER IN 150 YEARS

- The great freeze of 1962-3 -

Some of the lowest temperatures and heaviest snowfalls for 150 years were recorded during the winter of 1962-3.[29] The last time it had been this cold was in 1814 – the year before Napoleon met his Waterloo.

In Bristol the snow started falling on the afternoon of 26 December. During the evening, as people settled to watch the customary Boxing Day viewing on a TV – a Brian Rix farce, followed by a youthful Brian Blessed in *Z Cars* – blizzard conditions gently brought the city to a halt. For a few days over the festive season the Siberian anticyclone was something to enjoy. It was a time of snowball fights in the streets and sledging in the parks. But after a brief respite conditions got worse.

1962-3. It was a constant battle to keep Bristol's hilly roads free of snow and ice. A policeman and public-spirited bystanders give a van a push up Blackboy Hill. © Bristol Post.

The great freeze of 1962-3. The docks froze over. In places the ice was 10 centimetres thick. © Bristol Post.

By Boxing Day 1962, Bristol was brought to a halt by blizzard conditions. Bristol Bridge, with the tower of St Mary-le-Port and the new Norwich Union building in the background. © Bristol Post.

On 29 December blizzards resumed, driven by gale force winds.

The South West of England bore the brunt of the storm. Traffic shuddered to a standstill. All train services were cancelled as lines were blocked by snow and points froze. Two trains were buried under snow at Yate, and at Ston Easton, in the Mendips, a coach party was stranded for 24 hours. On country lanes the snow drifted to the hedge tops. There were drifts six metres deep.

Over the next 90 days there were numerous fresh falls of snow with daytime temperatures rarely above freezing. In the bitter cold the docks froze over; in places the pack ice was 10 centimetres thick. The Aust Ferry was cancelled for seven days due to potential damage from mini-icebergs floating down the Severn.

It was a constant battle to keep Bristol's hilly roads free of snow and ice. As people shivered back to work the streets rang to the sound of shovels. A team of over 1,000 council workers, requisitioned from departments made inoperable by the adverse weather, was tasked with clearing the streets. The ice was then tipped from trucks into the Cut.

As the weeks went by there was alarm that local stocks of coal, the primary method of domestic heating, would run out. Mickleburgh's music shop on Stokes Croft generously offered old pianos to be broken up for fuel. Meanwhile, in the days before most people had central heating, pipes froze overnight and some had to resort to boiling snow for their water. The price of carrots, cabbages and other fresh vegetables shot up. For many, the misery of this mini ice-age was made even worse by the cancellation of ten weeks of football matches. The football season was extended, again and again.

When the thaw eventually arrived over 5,000 council properties were affected by burst pipes.

The snow didn't fully clear until the end of March.

THE WRATH OF GOD

- *Earthquakes* -

At the risk of tempting fate, the likelihood of a major earthquake in Bristol is small. The British Geological Society, nevertheless, states that 200-300 earthquakes occur every year in the UK. Major earthquakes happen when tectonic plates move: the nearest of which is far away in the mid-Atlantic. The risk of a tsunami is another matter though!

Smaller tremors, due to minor adjustments in the earth's crust, do take place every year or so. They usually cause little or no damage, merely vibrating windows and rattling cupboards.

In 1232 it was written: 'this year was a great wind and earthquake with thunder and lightnings'. This sounds an unlikely coincidence of earthquake AND thunderstorm. More feasible is that the hammer of thunder felt like an earthquake.

The Dover Straits earthquake, which was felt in Bristol, is one of the largest UK earthquakes recorded in history. 'Thursday in Easter week 1580 there was a great earthquake in London, Bristol and Sarum and many other places of this realm, which made many people sore afraid.'[30]

In past times natural, but unusual, events such as an earth tremor, an aurora borealis or a comet, were viewed as a sign of the wrath of God and a bad omen. After the Dover Straits earthquake a spate of pamphlets published in London exhorted people to reform their sinful ways.

An earthquake was felt in Bristol on 4 March 1691, but this was nothing compared with the after-effects of the great Lisbon earthquake of 1755, when much of the Portuguese city was destroyed by tremor and then fire. Shock-waves were felt as far away as Finland. A three metre tsunami hit the Cornish coast, while it was reported that the water of the Hotwell Spa turned red and was undrinkable for several days.

ENDNOTES

1   Horton, B. *West Country Weather Book*, 1995, Barry Horton.
2   Matthews, W. *Bristol Directory*, 1793, Bristol, (facsimile edition) p.1.
3   ibid, p.3.
4   Bettey,J.H., *Bristol Observed*, 1986, Redcliffe, p.68.
5   ibid, p.77.
6   Defoe, D., *A tour through the island of Great Britain*, 1779, p.239.
7   *Arrowsmiths Dictionary of Bristol*, 1906, Bristol, p.107.
8   https://www.theguardian.com/environment/2019/nov/18/air-pollution-kills-bristol-health. Accessed 09/02/2020.
9   Lord, J. & Southam, J., *The Floating Harbour*, 1983, Redcliffe, p.38.
10   ibid., p.38.
11   Moss, B.S., Canon of Bristol Cathedral, 1960-66. (My father-in-law!) Verbatim discussion with the author.
12   https://www.gatheringvoices.org.uk/post/feeder-canal. Accessed 13 June 2021.
13   Bristol Times and Mirror, *Work in Bristol*, 1883, p.31.
14   Reid, H., *Bristol & Co*, 1987, Redcliffe Press, p.99.
15   Diaper, S. in Harvey, C. & Press, J., Ed, *Studies in the Business History of Bristol*, 1988, Bristol Academic Press, p.40.
16   Anon, *Bristol as WE remember it*, undated, Bristol Broadsides, p.16.

17   Diaper, S. in Harvey, C. & Press, J., op. cit., p.34.
18   Seyer, S., *Memoirs Historical and Topographical of Bristol*, 1823, Bristol, p.57.
19   Evans, J., *A Chronological Outline of the History of Bristol*, 1824, Bristol, p.164.
20   Seyer, S., op cit. p.514.
21   ibid., p.536.
22   Evans, J., op. cit., p.252
23   Clarke, G.T., *Report to the General Board of Health*, 1850, London, p.83.
24   Stone, G.F., *Bristol As It Was and As It Is*, 1909, Walter Reid, p.314.
25   Ralph, E. *Government of Bristol 1373-1973*, 1973, Bristol Corporation, p.37.
26   Horton, B. *West Country Weather Book*, 1995, Bristol, p.108 -18.
27   Anon., *The Northern Foul Water Interceptor*, Undated brochure (1994?), Bristol.
28   *Adam's Chronicle of Bristol*, 1910, Bristol. Adams's Chronicle contains an annual list of magistrates and a brief idiosyncratic account of what happened each year. It covers the period 1216-1639.
29   Much of the information about the winter of 1962-3 has been drawn from Barry Horton's fascinating *West Country Weather Book* (1995).
30   Seyer, S., op. cit., p.249.

REALISTS AND ROMANTICS

LITERARY SUPERSTAR

- Hannah More -

In her day Hannah More (1745-1833) was a literary superstar, admired by royalty and feted by fellow contemporary authors. She was a celebrated poet, playwright and campaigner for the rights of women, the abolition of slavery and the extension of education. Her pamphlets were distributed by the million and widely translated, not only into European languages but also into more geographically remote parlance such as Persian, Tamil and Singhalese.

Hannah More was born in 1745 in accommodation adjoining the school in Fishponds where her father taught. She followed the family tradition of teaching, joining her four sisters at their *School for Young Ladies* at 6, Trinity Street, College Green – soon to be re-located to the newly built Park Street at number 43. Her first play *The Search after Happiness* was performed when she was only 17-years-old.[1]

More was a woman of strong and sometimes contradictory views. She supported women's rights, yet was a critic of Mary Wollstonecraft's

Hannah More.

Hannah More was a celebrated poet, playwright and campaigner for the rights of women, the abolition of slavery and the extension of education.

Hannah More was born in 1745 in the adjoining accommodation to the school in Fishponds where her father taught.

Vindication of the Rights of Woman (1792); she was an internationalist while at the same time being a francophobe.

After a timid older admirer left More the substantial annuity of £200 a year she was able to give up teaching and move to London to concentrate on writing.[2] She was a charismatic networker. A list of her friends and acquaintances reads like an 18th century *Who's Who*: Walpole; Sheridan; Garrick; Pope and Joshua Reynolds to name but a few. Though grumpy old Dr Samuel Johnson had trouble coping with her enthusiasm.

In her late 30s More sought a quieter, more idyllic life in Somerset. First, she moved to Cowslip Green, then to the more substantial Barley Wood, both near Wrington. Yet More's popularity continued. A visit to her house was an obligatory excursion for any dilettante staying at the Hotwells or in Bath. She received a constant stream of pilgrims including Coleridge, Southey, and the opium-eating Thomas De Quincy.

More never lost her desire to teach. With evangelical zeal she set up Sunday and day

In her late 30s Hannah More sought a quieter, more idyllic life in Somerset. Bust in the porch of the Church of All Saints, Wrington.

In 1827 Hannah More moved back to Bristol and spent the last days of her life in Windsor Terrace, Clifton.

schools that taught basic reading and writing to farm labourers, coal miners and glass workers in the North Somerset villages. The acquisition of such key skills could life changing.

In 1827 More moved back to Bristol and spent the last days of her life in Windsor Terrace, Clifton. She died in 1833 at the age of 88. A writer and educator of courage and conviction, she burned bright in a world where there were few opportunities for women. Today, her star has sunk. Although one of the most successful authors of her time, all her works are now out of print.

This literary superstar's name lives on in Hannah More Primary School, St Philips.

Ann Yearsley (1752-1806)

Ann Yearsley was known as the milkwoman poet. Yearsley was mentored by Hannah More, who was charmed by her poetry and naive manner. More wrote: 'Ann is 8 and 20, slender and not ill-made; her face plain, but not disagreeable, her countenance rather pensive than sad, her pronunciation vulgar and provincial, but her taste uncommonly accurate and her sentiments very noble'.[3]

Her skill as a poet aside, it was largely thanks to More's social connections that Yearsley was able to secure a substantial publishing deal.

Yearsley didn't take well to being over-patronised. The relationship between the two women soured when Yearsley asked for her £500 advance – rather than have More retain the royalties for safekeeping.

Yearsley was unfairly labelled an 'ingrate' and the famous admirers drifted away. Meanwhile, with her money, Yearsley set up a subscription library at the Hotwells.[4] The library was not a success and it is said – probably by her detractors – that Yearsley died insane. 'Her progress towards oblivion

Ann Yearsley, the milkwoman poet.

was as rapid as it appears to have been deserved.'[5] The message was clear: under no circumstances cross Hannah More. Without a patron and the consequent entrée into posh literary circles, the working-class milkwoman never stood a chance.

BRISTOL'S BOY POET – AND FORGER

- Thomas Chatterton (1752-70) -

Thomas Chatterton's gothic writing is an acquired taste. Chatterton became a tragic-romantic figure largely due to his depiction in Henry Wallis's (1830-1916) Pre-Raphaelite painting 'Death of Chatterton' that hangs in Tate Britain.

It is a large picture. A pallid faced young man, wearing striking peacock blue breeches, lies stretched-out on a bed, below an open attic window. Through the window is the dome of St Pauls; on the

Chatterton became a romantic figure largely due to Henry Wallis's (1830-1916) painting 'Death of Chatterton' that hangs in Tate Britain. © Tate.

floor are pieces of paper torn up like confetti. The 17-year-old Chatterton is dead.

Chatterton was the epitome of the starving poet in a garret. He wasn't a popular child in Bristol. 'Too clever for his own good,' they said. The feeling was mutual. Chatterton wrote scathingly 'hardly twenty in the town could read'. He was a single child brought up by a

Chatterton's house in the shadow of St Mary Redcliffe.

widowed mother. His father, a school teacher, died a couple of months before he was born. Chatterton lived in the shadow of St Mary Redcliffe – his house still stands, stranded by the dual carriageway opposite the church.[6]

He left school at 14 and went to work as a clerk in Corn Street.[7] His tasks were undemanding and left him with plenty of spare time. He would spend these quiet moments experimenting with, and developing, his own unique writing style.

At the same instant, William Barrett (1733-89), a surgeon, resolved to write a history of his home city. It was quite a task. Nobody had written a comprehensive account of Bristol before. Barrett studied documents and charters in the Council House – at that time on the corner of Corn Street and Broad Street – and visited the city's library in King Street. He also sought out documents in private hands.

Chatterton claimed he had access to the archives of St Mary Redcliffe, held in a store room above the north porch.

It was an ambitious venture. Barrett put out the word across the city. Documents came flooding in. But there were still gaps. The young Chatterton got news of the project and offered to help.

Chatterton claimed he had access to the archives of St Mary Redcliffe, which were held in a store room above the north porch. Among all the dusty ecclesiastical books and manuscripts were the writings of a medieval monk, Rowley. Chatterton copied extracts from Rowley's original manuscripts and gave them to Barrett. Barrett was overjoyed – this was new and original material that had never been seen before.

Soon after, the young Chatterton, disillusioned with the lack of opportunities for a poetic genius in Bristol, caught the daily coach to London. Coming from a single parent family with few connections, the likelihood of fame and fortune was slim. Four months later Chatterton was dead; buried in a pauper's grave.[8]

The coroner's verdict was suicide while 'non compus mentis'. However, it is also speculated that his death was accidental and that he died from a lethal cocktail of arsenic

Magnum Opus

Barrett's *magnum opus*, the first complete history of Bristol, was eventually published to acclaim in 1789. *The History and Antiquities of the City of Bristol* was a massive 704 page tome, accompanied by specially commissioned illustrations and a detailed fold-out map.

But Barrett's moment of glory was short lived. Chatterton's manuscripts were said to be forgeries and the humiliated historian became discredited. Barrett's life-work was exposed as flawed. It is said that, in a fury, he tore out the offending phoney pages from the unsold books. Barrett died later that same year.

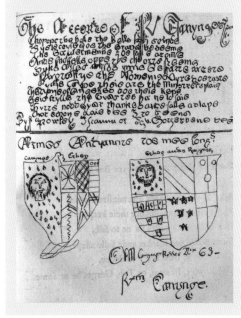

and opium taken to relieve the symptoms of syphilis.[9]

After his death in 1777 Chatterton's Rowley Poems were published in a 308-page volume. It was an extraordinary achievement for a 17-year-old.

A BROAD DIALECT

- *The Bristol accent* -

In 1770 Thomas Chatterton felt it necessary to move to London to develop his writing career. Times were changing, however. The editors of Daniel Defoe's *A tour through the island of Great Britain* (1779), found that Bristol had altered almost beyond recognition with regards to the arts. They commented that there was now an element of culture to be found in the city: 'Literature and genteel education are much cultivated in Bristol; and it abounds with agreeable women whose modes of dress are universally approved'. They also noted: 'Its gentry, merchants and capital traders are polite and superb in their town and country houses, equipages, servants and amusements as any in the Kingdom'.[10]

One thing still rankled though. Behind all this finery the Bristol accent could not be disguised. Although Defoe's guide admitted that 'People of rank and education here, as everywhere else, pronounce with propriety' it conceded that other members of the trading classes spoke in a `broad dialect much worse than the common people in the metropolis, though they are not willing to acknowledge it.'[11]

Today, the most distinguishing feature of the Bristol accent is the addition of a final 'L' to words ending in a vowel. Consequently, area, becomes '*areal*', idea becomes *ideal* and America becomes *Americal*. Bristol's motto was memorably changed by West Country singer, Adge Cutler (1930-74), to Virtute et Industrial.

- *Churz Drive!* -
Some Bristol words [12]

Blige! – expression of surprise
Daps – plimsolls
Drive – bus driver
Gurt – big, large
Macky – large
Munter – unattractive
Pitching – snow settling
Scrage – scab
Slider – play equipment
Smoothing – stroking, ie smoothing the cat.
Spinner – liar
Toppers – end crusts of a loaf of bread.

A NEW POETIC MOVEMENT

- Coleridge (and Wordsworth) in Bristol -

It was during the last decade of the 18th century that Bristol became the birthplace of a new literary movement: Romanticism.

The great romantic poets of the era, Samuel Taylor Coleridge (1772-1834), Robert Southey (1774-1843) and William Wordsworth (1770-1850) all spent time in Bristol in the 1790s.

In 1795, the young poet William Wordsworth was a guest of plantation owner John Pinney (1740-1818) at his residence in Great George Street – now the Georgian House Museum. Here, he met Coleridge for the first time. It must surely have been an interesting gathering – Coleridge, the ardent abolitionist, in the house of a plantation owner using enslaved workers! The meeting did, however, lead to a lifelong friendship between Coleridge and Wordsworth, and a ground-breaking collaboration: the compilation of the influential *Lyrical Ballads.*

Coleridge had been encouraged to move to Bristol by his friend, the future Poet Laureate, Robert Southey. Coleridge and Southey shared lodgings in College Street, behind what is now City Hall.[13]

Here, they hatched a proto-hippie plan, part of the idealism that was sweeping Europe after the French Revolution, to establish a commune in North America. The awkwardly named Pantisocratic Scheme was to involve a group of like-minded artists who would labour a mere three or four hours a day before devoting the remainder of their time to creative endeavours. A crucial element of the scheme was that each communard – they were all men – should take 'a mild and lovely young woman for his wife'.

The daughters of the recently widowed Mrs Fricker of Redcliffe Hill became a magnet for these excitable poets. Coleridge wed Sara Fricker in 1795, Southey married Edith, while the ailing Robert Lovell (1771-96) (a lesser known poet) was already married to Mary. Martha, a younger, but wiser, Fricker sister, turned down the literary dilettante, George Burnet, realising he only wanted 'a wife in a hurry'.

Meanwhile, Wordsworth, who had been in France and seen the French revolution at first hand, wasn't part of the commune plan. For female company he enjoyed the companionship of his sister, Dorothy,

Coleridge's life with Sara could not be described as happy. They married in a blur of idealism. With time the haze cleared, yet, to Coleridge's dismay, the marriage bonds remained. Coleridge was not easy to live with. Even in these early days he was addicted to laudanum, the alcoholic tincture of opium, and consequently was subject to unpredictable extremes of mood. Sara was also the victim of character assassination among Coleridge's literary contemporaries. The poet Shelley was to maliciously observe of the Fricker sisters: 'Mrs Southey is stupid; Mrs Coleridge worse'.

While waiting for converts to the Pantisocratic scheme, Coleridge busied himself by writing radical lectures which, for a small fee, he would deliver at various inns across the city. Although his talk of revolution and the abolition of the slave trade was rarely passively received he was well able to defend himself against hecklers with acid wit. On one occasion a hostile audience expressed their disapproval by hissing. Coleridge retorted:

'I am not at all surprised that when the red hot prejudices are plunged into cold water they should go off with a hiss.'

His audiences were not impressed by his dishevelled appearance. A local journal wrote:

'His speech is a perfect monotonism, his person is slovenly . . . Mr Coleridge would do well to appear in cleaner stockings and if his hair were combed out every time he appeared in public it would not deprecate him in the esteem of his friends'.[14]

Samuel and Sarah Coleridge moved to a small earth-floored cottage in Nether Stowey, Somerset. Now much improved.

Coleridge also dabbled in journalism, publishing a political rag called the *Watchman*. The journal, whose strap line was 'That all may know the truth and that the truth may make us free'[15] was written to promote free speech – which was currently under threat due to the so-called 'Gagging Acts' of 1795. After ten issues Coleridge ran out of enthusiasm for the project and the paper folded. Coleridge elegized, 'O Watchman thou hast watched in vain'.

Undaunted by the lack of converts for the commune and the failure of the magazine, Coleridge turned his attention to something that was to be of more lasting value: the production of his first book of poems. Prior to his arrival in Bristol, Coleridge had submitted works to various publishers in London. The best advance to be offered was six guineas. Impoverished though he was, the poet was not willing to accept such a derisory fee.

In Bristol, however, the publisher and bookseller Joseph Cottle (1770-1853), with premises in the High Street, promised a healthy advance of £30. There were times when Cottle regretted his benevolence. Coleridge's procrastination could try even the most patient. Coleridge was a larger than life figure. He was bold, talkative, generous and fun to be with, but he could also be self-obsessed and annoyingly whimsical. Cottle was repeatedly obliged to remind the poet of his commitment. In return Coleridge sent notes to his publisher explaining his tardiness. His messages ranged from the optimistic: 'I have been composing in the fields this morning' to dramatic excuses: 'A devil, a very devil, has got possession of my left temple, eye, cheek, jaw and shoulder . . . I write in agony'.

Coleridge's first volume of poetry was eventually published in April 1796. It proved Coleridge to be a serious writer and paved the way for the works of genius that were to follow.

In March 1797 Samuel and Sara Coleridge left their 'pent up rooms' on Redcliffe Hill and moved briefly to Oxford Street in Kingsdown. Shortly after, the Coleridges retreated to a small earth-floored cottage in the village of Nether Stowey in Somerset where Samuel continued his search for beauty, truth and liberty.

In 1798, Cottle published a joint volume of poetry by Coleridge and Wordsworth, the ground-breaking *Lyrical Ballads. Lyrical Ballads* contained, among other pieces, Coleridge's *The Rime of the Ancient Mariner* and Wordsworth's sublime *Lines written a few miles above Tintern Abbey.* This new romantic poetry wasn't to everybody's taste. Sarah Coleridge wrote: 'the lyrical ballads are not liked at all by anyone'.[16] Time has proved

What was Romanticism?

The late 18th century was a time of unprecedented change. Industrialisation was well underway; there were increasing demands for politics to become more democratic; the arts were becoming more accessible. Romanticism was a reaction to the lofty, classical impersonal themes of previous times. Poetry was to be more accessible. It was to be deeply felt, focusing on the charm of everyday life, of nature and the familiar.

otherwise.

In 1813, Coleridge returned briefly to Bristol to deliver further lectures.[17] By this time he was suffering from ill health and opium addiction. From 1816, Coleridge took refuge in the house of his physician, Dr Gillman, in Highgate, London. He stayed there until his death in 1834.

SOME BRISTOL LITERARY CONNECTIONS

Angela Carter (1940-92)

Angela Carter, who moved to Bristol in 1961 and lived in Royal York Crescent, is widely regarded as one of the most influential writers of the 20th century. Her novels, *Shadow of Dance*, *Several Perceptions* and *Love,* often dubbed the Bristol Trilogy, are set in the city. Her unique gothic vision of a rundown Bristol in the 1960s is otherworldly and mildly disturbing.

Robinson Crusoe

Daniel Defoe's (1660-1731) story of Robinson Crusoe is said to be based on the exploits of Alexander Selkirk who was rescued from the Pacific island of Juan Fernandez in 1709 by Bristol captain and privateer Woodes Rogers, resident of Queen Square.

Helen Dunmore (1952-2017)

Novelist, short story writer and poet, Dunmore lived in Bristol for over 30 years. Her last novel, *Birdcage Walk*, was set in 18th century Bristol. It posthumously won the Costa Poetry and Book of the Year Award.

Eca de Queiroz (1845-1900)

The famous Portuguese novelist, Eca de Queiroz lived in Stoke Bishop for some ten years while he was Portuguese Consul in the City. He wasn't enamoured with Britain: 'Everything about this society is disagreeable to me – from its limited way of thinking to its indecent manner of cooking vegetables.'[18]

Christopher Fry (1907-2005)

Author of the play *The Lady's Not for Burning*, the title of which was later turned into one of Margaret Thatcher's catch phrases, lived in Sefton Park Road, St Andrews. Born Christopher Fry Harris, he was a close friend of T.S. Eliot and was one of the writers, along with Gore Vidal, of the screenplay for *Ben-Hur*.

Allen Lane (1902-70)

The man who changed the face of publishing by inventing the paperback, was born in Bristol, lived in Cotham Walk and was educated at Bristol Grammar School. It is said that he conceived the idea of the Penguin paperback in 1935 when, returning from Agatha Christie's home in Devon, he was stranded on Exeter station with nothing of quality to read.[19] The Penguin Archive is held by the University of Bristol.

Dr Peter Roget (1779-1869)

Wordsmith Dr Peter Roget, the eponymous author of *Roget's Thesaurus,* spent a year in his early 20s working with Thomas Beddoes at the Pneumatic Institute in Dowry Square (See *Manson's Bristol Miscellany*, Volume 1, p.112-3.[20])

Samuel Pepys (1633-1703)

In June 1668, the great diarist Samuel Pepys, who was staying in Bath, took an excursion to Bristol where his maid (and secret lover) Deb Willet was brought up. After visiting a barber to be shaved, Pepys walked through the city which he described as: '...in every respect another London that one can hardly know it to stand in the country...' Pepys dined at Deb Willet's parent's house '...a substantial good house and well-furnished and did give us good entertainment of strawberries, a whole venison pasty cold and plenty of brave wine and above all bristoll milk'.[21]

Robert Louis Stevenson (1850-94)

In R. L. Stevenson's classic adventure story *Treasure Island*, young Jim Hawkins briefly wanders through an atmospheric, but geographically inexact, dockside Bristol on his way to meet Long John Silver at the Spy-glass Inn. It has been claimed that the Spy-glass was modelled on The Hole in the Wall next to Queen Square, while the Llandoger Trow in King Street was the inspiration for the Admiral Benbow.

The Long John Silver Trail (www.longjohnsilvertrust.co.uk) tells the story of Bristol's connections with Treasure Island *and its maritime past.*

Robert Southey (1774-1843)

Born in Wine Street in 1774, Southey is Bristol's only English Poet Laureate. He held the post for 30 years. He was a prolific writer and poet. He is best known for his biography of *Nelson* and the children's classic *The Story of Goldilocks and the Three Bears*!

Joyce Storey (1917-2001)

Began writing at the age of 66. Her vivid tales of a working-class woman's life in Bristol were first issued by the Bristol Broadsides collective. She was able to reach a wider audience when she was published by Virago Press in 1992.

E.H. Young (1880-1949)

Emily Hilda Young was born in Northumberland but moved to Bristol in 1902. She was a best-selling author in the 1920s but is now largely forgotten. She lived in a flat in Saville Place, Clifton, between 1907-18 and wrote a series of novels set in Upper Radstowe – a thinly disguised Clifton. Young was an active suffragist and a pioneer of women's rock climbing.[22]

Comic masterpieces

Two comic masterpieces, *Three Men in a Boat* (1889) and the *Diary of a Nobody* (1892) were both first published by Bristol printer, J.W. Arrowsmith. At the time of their publication neither books were a critical or financial success. Even so, *Three Men in a Boat* by Jerome K. Jerome (1858-1927) went on to sell over three million English language copies and has been widely translated.[23]

When not producing bestsellers, Arrowsmith's core business was publishing railway and steamship timetables.

'VERY LITTLE CHANCE OF BECOMING KING'

- Hollywood beckons -

Spending your early years in Bristol is certainly no bar to becoming a Hollywood superstar. The important thing is to make sure you leave the city.

Cary Grant (1904-65)

Cary Grant, the suavest of Hollywood actors, was born Alexander Archibald Leach. His early childhood was spent at 15 Hughenden Road, Horfield. But he moved to Picton Street, Montpelier, to live with his 'nan' when his mother was temporarily incarcerated in Glenside mental asylum. Grant was a pupil at Fairfield School.

Bob Hope (1903-2003)

This most American of all comedians spent his earliest days playing in St George's Park. Born in London, his family moved to Chalks Road, Redfield, before emigrating – 'because I knew I had very little chance of becoming king' – two years later to Ohio, USA,[24] In 1952, he returned to Bristol to visit his childhood home.

Deborah Kerr (1921-2007)

Known to the film world as the 'English rose', Kerr was born in Glasgow in 1921. She was educated at Northumberland House boarding school, Henleaze. As well as studying ballet, she caught the bug for performing from her aunt Jane who helped run the Hicks-Smale Drama School in Redland, overlooking the Downs.

Kerr hit the Hollywood big time after starring in *From Here to Eternity* (1953). Her passionate romp in the breaking waves with Burt Lancaster is one of the most memorable beach scenes in the history of the cinema. Kerr took the female lead in another blockbuster, the musical, *The King and I* (1956), though her singing was over-dubbed by the well-known session vocalist, Marni Nixon. In 1957 Kerr co-starred with Horfield mega-star Cary Grant in *An Affair to Remember* where they were nominated for four Oscars.[25]

Sir Thomas Lawrence (1769-1830)

Born in Redcross Street, 'Tommy', as he was known locally, was a child prodigy. During his teenage years he was painting portraits of high society. By the age of 20 he had been commissioned to undertake a portrait of King George III's wife, Queen Charlotte (1744-1818). The Prince Regent commissioned Lawrence to paint studies of Britain's allied leaders after the Napoleonic Wars. In 1820 Lawrence became president of the Royal Academy.

The exterior of Lawrence's house in Redcross Street survives in what must be the most unsympathetic development in Bristol.

'A LARGE AND IN EVERY WAY EXCELLENT LIBRARY'

- The City Library -

'One of the most outstanding contributions to the cultural life of the city was the development of the public library system...'[26]

B ristol had one of the oldest public libraries in the country.

In 1613, a free public library 'for merchants and shopkeepers', was founded by Robert Redwood, who donated his lodge by the city wall (later King Street, laid out in the 1650s) for that purpose.[27] The library was extended in 1640, and then completely rebuilt in 1743.[28] The west wing was added in 1786. Many of the books were so precious that they were chained to the shelves to avoid pilfering.

Somehow, in 1773, control of the City Library was hi-jacked by the Bristol Library Society who turned the King Street establishment into an exclusive male-only subscription library. For the following 80 years access to this important collection of books was limited to a clique of misogynists who could afford the fees.

Nevertheless, one of the subscribers, Samuel Taylor Coleridge, described the institution as 'a large and in every way excellent library.' The registers that recorded Coleridge and Robert Southey's loans are still preserved.

Matthews, in his 1793 *Directory*, wrote that the library contained 'a copious and excellent collection of ancient and modern authors which are perpetually increasing due to donations and subscriptions'.[29]

Libraries are powerful symbols of a belief in the right to free thought and distribution of knowledge. During the 19th century a number of Library Acts authorised local authorities

The original 1740 library in King Street.

Old Library, King Street, in a bad state of repair in the 1930s.

to provide free public libraries funded through local taxes.[30] In 1854 Bristol Council became officially responsible for libraries.[31] It consequently wrestled back control of the King Street library from the misogynistic Bristol

Library Society in 1855.

By 1905 there were ten new libraries in Bristol:[32]

- Central Library, King Street, 1613.
- St Philip's Library, Trinity Road, 1876.
- Cheltenham Road Library, 1877.
- Bedminster Library, 1877.
- Redland Library, Whiteladies Road, 1885.
- Hotwells Library, Clifton Wood, 1888.
- Avonmonuth Library, 1896.
- St George Library, Church Road, 1899.
- Fishponds Library, 1900.
- Shirehampton Library, 1905.

The Council even had its own book bindery, based in the Cheltenham Road Library, to bind and repair the library books.

The original Central Library in King Street is now a restaurant.

BANKSY

- Bristol's favourite scoundrel -

I can't write a book on Bristol without mentioning the city's most favourite scoundrel-turned-hero.

Banksy first came to notice in the 1990s as an annoying young man who fanatically stencilled his name on walls, billboards and buildings (and cows) around Bristol. Within hours of the statue of Neptune being boarded-up in preparation for the Millennium celebrations, Banksy's name miraculously appeared stencilled across it. He slowly entered the public consciousness. A little book *Existencilism* was published and went on sale at the Arnolfini; *Greenleaf Bookshop* sold Banksy prints for the (then) exorbitant price of £60. They are now worth thousands of pounds.

The turning point was an exhibition at Severnshed in 2000 when the full range and humour of Banksy's work was publically on display. Some of the artwork sold for a staggering £750. Banksy was not just a graffiti vandal, he was now an artist.

Banksy generated an interesting debate. The city council held a referendum when a Banksy stencil was cheekily applied in 2006 to the wall of a building at the bottom of Park Street directly opposite City Hall. The public deemed this was a work of art and should not be removed. Tourists began to visit Bristol to view Banksy murals and other street art in and around the Stokes Croft area.

Suddenly everybody loved Banksy. Young and old queued for hours for the Banksy exhibition in 2009 at the City Museum and Art Gallery. Banksy, the former vandal, rescued the

Suddenly everybody loved Banksy. Young and old queued for hours for the Banksy exhibition in 2009 at the City Museum and Art Gallery.

The Mild Mild West, Banksy.

city from economic recession! He generated £16 million pounds of visitor income. Banksy was a global phenomenon and had put Bristol on the map.

So who is Banksy? Those who claim to know him, call him Robin. But you don't want to know. You wouldn't want to unmask Zorro, would you?

GILL SANS – THE TYPEFACE OF CHOICE

- Eric Gill -

The famous Gill Sans typeface was first used on the fascia of a Bristol bookshop in 1928. Sculptor and typographer Eric Gill (1882-1940) had experimented on a sans serif typeface while he was living at the Capel y Finn Monastery in the Black Mountains. The new typeface appeared on a sign for Douglas Cleverdon's bookshop on Park Street.[33] It was soon to become the typeface of choice for the BBC, Penguin book covers and the Church of England.

Gill Sans Light
ABCDEFGHIJKLMNOPQRSTUVWXYZ
abcdefghijklmnopqrstuvwxyz
0123456789

Gill Sans Semi Bold
ABCDEFGHIJKLMNOPQRSTUVWXYZ
abcdefghijklmnopqrstuvwxyz
0123456789

Gill Sans Regular
ABCDEFGHIJKLMNOPQRSTUVWXYZ
abcdefghijklmnopqrstuvwxyz
0123456789

Gill Sans Bold
ABCDEFGHIJKLMNOPQRSTUVWXYZ
abcdefghijklmnopqrstuvwxyz
0123456789

ENDNOTES

1   Hutton, S., *Bristol and its Famous Associations*, 1907, Arrowsmith, p.85-95.
2   ibid., p.87.
3   Waldron, M., *Lactilla, Milkwoman of Clifton*, 1996, University of Georgia Press, p. 58.
4   Duffus, J. *The Women Who Built Bristol*, 2018, Tangent, p.406-7.
5   Hutton, S., *op. cit.*, p.97.
6   ibid., p.53-81.
7   Cottle, B., *Chatterton*, in Ed McGrath, P., *Bristol in the 18th Century*, 1972, David and Charles, p.95.
8   ibid., p.105.
9   Groom, N., *The Death of Chatterton*, in Heys, A. *From Gothic to Romantic: Thomas Chatterton's Bristol*, 2005, Redcliffe Press, p.115-25.
10 Defoe, D., *A tour through the island of Great Britain*, 1779, p.239.
11 ibid., p.239.
12 Stoke, H. & Green,V., *A Dictionary of Bristol*, 2013, Tangent Books.
13 Hutton, S., *op. cit.*, p.108.
14 Carpenter, M. *The Indifferent Horseman*, 1954, Elek Books, p.63.
15 Coleridge, S.T., *The Watchman*, Issue 1, 1 March 1796, p.1.
16 Hutton, S., *op. cit.*, p.124.
17 Holmes, R., *Coleridge – Darker Reflections*, 1998, Harper Collins, p.343
18 https://en.wikipedia.org/wiki/Jos%C3%A9_Maria_de_E%C3%A7a_de_Queir%C3%B3s
19 Lowery, H., *Bristol Review of Books*, Issue 3, Spring 2007, p.4.
20 Hutton, S., *op. cit.*, p.118.
21 Bettey, J.H., *Bristol Observed*, 1986, Redcliffe Press, p.55.
22 Duffus, J., *op. cit.*, p.408.
23 Reid, H., *Bristol & Co*, 1987, Redcliffe Press, p.78.
24 http://news.bbc.co.uk/1/hi/entertainment/showbiz/198932.stm
25 My thanks to Mark Steeds for this information about Deborah Kerr.
26 Meller, H. E., *Leisure and the Changing City, 1870-1914*, 1976, Routledge Keegan Paul, p.101.
27 Anon., *Arrowsmith's Dictionary of Bristol*, 1906, Arrowsmith, p.237.
28 Evans, J. *A Chronological Outline of the History of Bristol*, 1824, p. 291.
29 Matthews, W., *New History of Bristol and Complete Guide*, 1793, facsimile edition, p.82.
30 Meller, H. E., *op. cit.*, p.101.
31 Bush, G., *Bristol and its Municipal Government, 1820-51*, 1976, Bristol Record Society, p.210.
32 Anon., *Arrowsmith's Dictionary of Bristol*, 1906, Arrowsmith, p.238.
33 Garfield, S., *Just My Type*, 2010, Profile Books, p.49.

A ROOF OVER YOUR HEAD

'HERE WE SPEND OUR AGE'

- Almshouses -

Freed from all storms the tempest and the rage
Of billows, here we spend our age.
Our weather beaten vessels here repair
And from the merchants' kind and generous care
Find harbour here; no more we put to sea
Until we launch into Eternity...
Extract from a verse on Merchants' Almshouses, King Street.

'The greatness of a city should be measured by its benefice rather than its wealth', wrote J.F. Nicholls (1818-83), the Bristol historian and city librarian, in 1875.

How to support the poor – or not – is an eternal and universal question. Throughout history there have been cycles of economic boom and slump and through no fault of their own people have found themselves out of work and unable to pay rent.

The origins of Bristol's almshouses date back 700 years. Before the days of state welfare almshouses were established to give housing and relief to the deserving poor. Almshouses were originally considered as homes for life. Places were much sought-after. Residents would frequently receive a small pension plus other allowances such as coal and clothing. It was the golden ticket.

Thus, in 1679, Alderman Stevens endowed a charity 'to provide almshouses and other housing for poor persons of good character resident in Bristol'. Most almshouses would have a chapel attached where the residents would pray to God and also for the soul of the founder.

There are still a surprising number of almshouses dotted around Bristol. Over the centuries they have been updated and modernised many times, to meet changing needs.

Colston's Almshouses, St Michael's Hill.

St Nicholas with Burton's Almshouses, King Street.

SOME BRISTOL ALMSHOUSES

Barstaple Almshouses (Trinity South), Old Market Street. Founded in the 1390s by three times mayor of Bristol, John Barstaple. The building has been rebuilt a number of times. In 1881 '22 aged widowers'[1] lived there. It was sold in the 2000s. Residents were moved to purpose-built housing at Brentry.

Trinity Almshouses, Old Market Street. Founded by Isabella Barstaple, wife of John, in the 1390s. The current red brick building dates from 1913.

Foster's Almshouses, top of Christmas Steps. Founded by John Foster, 1483, rebuilt 1861-83, said to be modelled loosely on the Hotel De Dieu, Beaune. It has its own chapel, The Three Kings of Cologne. The almshouse has been sold and converted to private apartments.

Dr White's Almshouses, Bear Lane, between Temple Street and Temple Back. Founded in 1610 for six men and six women. Replaced in 1968 by the current almshouses in Prewitt Street, Redcliffe.

St Nicholas with Burton's Almshouses, King Street. Constructed in 1652 during the Commonwealth. In the courtyard, behind the almshouses, a section of the medieval city walls can be seen.

Alderman Stevens's Almshouses, Old Market Street. 1679. For 16 widows or daughters. Bombed 1941. The frontage on Old Market Street was replaced by a charmless and out-of-character 1960s building.

Colston's Almshouses, St Michael's Hill. Founded by Edward Colston, built 1691-6. For 12 men and 12 women. In addition to a small pension, each person would receive 12 sacks of coal a year. Still in the original building with its own chapel.

Merchant Venturers' Almshouses, King Street. 1696-99. The west side of the quadrangle was destroyed by bombing in 1941.

Merchants'Almshouses, King Street.

Lady Haberfield's Almshouse, Hotwell Road.
Erected in 1890. The once unrivalled view of the
harbour entrance lock is now brutally hidden by the
Cumberland Basin road system.

Merchant Taylors' Almshouses, Merchant Street. 1701. For seamen and seamen's widows. No longer an almshouse. Subsumed into the east end of the Galleries shopping complex.

Fry's House of Mercy, Colston Parade, Redcliffe. Founded 1778. Endowed by William Fry, a local distiller, it was built to house 12 widows.

Bengough's Almshouse, Horfield Road. Backing onto Colston's Almshouse. Founded by Henry Bengough in 1818 'as a perpetual place of refuge for the aged and infirm'. The most recent iteration designed by Foster and Wood in 1878. The almshouse became a care home in 1996 and was later converted into flats.

Lady Haberfield's Almshouse, Hotwell Road. Erected in 1890 [2], this is the last almshouse to be built in Bristol. Founded by Dame Sarah Haberfield (c.1800-1874) in memory of her husband, John Haberfield (1785-1857), six times mayor of Bristol. For 24 people of either sex. The once unrivalled view of the harbour entrance lock is now brutally hidden by the Cumberland Basin road system.

The buildings of Burton's, Dr Thomas White's, Ridley's and St Raphael's Almshouses were all victims of the Second World War blitz and not reconstructed.

Bristol's population:[3] [4]	
Mid-16th century	10,000
1600	12,000
1670	20,000
1700	30,000
1801	63,000
1851	159,000
1901	330,000
1931	397,000
1951	443,000
1971	428,000
2020	463,400

CHILDREN WOULD SLEEP SIX TO EIGHT IN A BED

- The Workhouse -

Mention of the workhouse struck fear into the hearts of generations of Bristolians. To end up in the workhouse was the dread of the poor and the elderly. What happened if, due to unforeseen and unfortunate circumstances, you could not work and had no family to support you? Where would you live? How would you pay the rent? The workhouse, the Dickensian harsh reality of the Victorian city, was for those who had hit rock-bottom and had nowhere else to go. It was better than sleeping under a hedgerow with a stone for a pillow – just.

In the Middle Ages, there might be accommodation in an almshouse for the elderly and infirm with a good track-record of church attendance and employment. But places were scarce. Otherwise, poor relief was mostly seen to be the responsibility of church institutions – of which there were plenty in and around Bristol.

With the dissolution of the monasteries in the 1540s, the parishes of Bristol were required to step-up and support the local poor. Ever mindful of costs, parishes would only give poor relief to their own parishioners. There was, however, always the suspicion that the able-bodied poor were lazy. Vagrant beggars, those of no fixed abode, would be whipped out of town.

1696 was a year of high unemployment largely due to a decline in the cloth trade. Bristol Corporation has the doubtful honour of setting up the first workhouse in England. Rather than each parish looking after its poor, a single workhouse was set up for the whole city.[5]

The cruelty and humiliation was almost unbelievable. It was like something out of a living nightmare. Officers responsible for apprehending vagrants would trawl the streets with a giant net stretched between two poles to capture these poor unfortunate men and women. They would then be taken to St Peter's Hospital, now repurposed as a workhouse, where they would be whipped and set to work.[6]

There was, at least, provision for the training of girls and boys. Girls were taught carding and spinning, while the boys wove 'fustians and calimancoes[7]'. The day to day regime in St Peter's workhouse was harsh and relentless. Disciplinary apparatus included stocks, a whipping post in the courtyard and a room for confinement with chains and fetterlocks.[8]

Additionally, in 1698, the Society of Friends established their own workhouse on River Street, next to the Frome, to support unemployed Quaker weavers.

Occasionally additional emergency support was needed. During the winter of 1710-11 there were several considerable falls of snow. Collections in all the parishes were made for the poor 'who were incapable of working because of the frost'.[9]

In 1832, a cholera epidemic hit Bristol and the inevitable happened. The workhouse was the epicentre of the outbreak. Of the 105 cases reported between 11 July and 10 August, 71 were in St. Peter's workhouse.[10] Such was the outrage at this sky-high death toll that a crowd gathered outside the workhouse and threatened to pull down the building.[11] There was also a rumour that the authorities were burying people alive. A mob broke into Temple churchyard and disinterred bodies to establish that they really were dead.[12]

The 1834 Poor Law Amendment Act ushered in a new national approach. The 1830s were disturbed times. A decline in agricultural jobs due to mechanisation had led to an increase in poverty and generated widespread political unrest. There was also agitation for wider voting rights. The recent Queen Square riot was a clear warning of how quickly matters could get out of hand. The unemployed and the angry needed to be controlled. The workhouse was the way to do this, and Bristol, with its St Peter's workhouse, already led the way.

Under the 1834 Act Bristol was divided into three areas, called Unions. Each Union was responsible for the running of a workhouse.

To minimise costs, the eminently unsuitable and rickety St Peter's continued to be used as a workhouse in central Bristol. The building was already dangerously over-crowded with 600 inmates. Children would sleep six to eight in a bed.[13] There were also wards set aside for so-called *lunatics* – some were confined in pens, while many women were masked or muzzled.

In an attempt to alleviate the overcrowding, additional accommodation was urgently sought. The moth-balled French Prison, out at Stapleton, last used in 1814, seemed to fit the bill. Without too many alterations the austere prison became a ready-made workhouse.

Meanwhile, the Bedminster Poor Law Union, responsible for paupers south of the

The Bedminster Poor Law Union, responsible for paupers south of the river, built a new workhouse, half a day's walk from Bristol, at Flax Bourton.

river, built a new workhouse, half a day's walk from Bristol, at Flax Bourton (1838). Finally, the Clifton Poor Law Union, which covered an arc of parishes across the north and east of the city, constructed a maze of ominously commanding buildings at Eastville. The Clifton Union also oversaw a number of smaller premises: for the aged and infirm in Clifton Wood; for children in St George and for the able-bodied in Pennywell Road.[14]

The humiliation continued. The new, purpose-built, workhouses had a penal flavour about them. Although the inhabitants were, in theory, free to leave, both of the workhouses were surrounded by high walls. Men, women and children were segregated into different blocks. There were also wards set aside for 'imbeciles'. This derogatory term was used to label those with learning difficulties or suffering from forms of dementia.

The conditions were deliberately harsh. There were workshops, and for male paupers, yards for manual work such as crushing bones or oakum picking.[15] The idea was to make the bread-line living of a labourer or farm worker appear attractive. The enforced work was monotonous; hygiene conditions were appalling. A reporter from the *British Medical Journal* in 1867 summed up his visit to the Flax Bourton Workhouse: '... the wards were crowded and badly ventilated. The water-closets were extremely foul. The lavatories were small and dirty; and there was no bath room attached to the infirmary.' The shocked reporter asked: 'Can it be possible that such an arrangement can be sanctioned by the Poor Law Board?'[16]

Outside relief continued for some. But those in receipt of relief were further humiliated by being required to wear a badge of red or blue cloth bearing the letter P as well as the initial letter of their parish.[17]

By the end of the 19th century, the cumbersome administration of the three unions, together with a more humane attitude toward the poor, meant that there were moves to consolidate the management of poor relief under one authority. The new Board of Guardians was formed in 1898. At that time there were over 11,000 people in Bristol under its care in orphanages, asylums, special schools and workhouses.[18] (The population of Bristol in 1901 was 330,000.)

The introduction of the social security system in 1912 saw the hesitant beginning of the end of the workhouse. Rather than stone breaking and bone crushing, more useful work creation schemes were devised. Already, the boating lake in Eastville Park had been dug as a job creation project during the winter of 1908-09. The construction of Muller Road and

Kellaway Avenue were also the product of similar schemes.[19]

Bristol's 'dole office', with separate entrances for Men, Women, Girls and Boys, opened in Nelson Street in 1931.[20]

Supporting senior citizens continued to be a challenge. A new workhouse at Southmead was set aside in 1904 for 'aged inmates of good character that did not need nursing'.[21] The Eastville workhouse, known as 101 Fishponds Road, also became a home for the 'aged poor' in the 1930s.

Flax Bourton workhouse building remains today. It has been rebranded as Farleigh Court and successfully adapted as a centre for small businesses. The Eastville workhouse was levelled in the 1980s and is now the site of a housing estate and flats; a plaque erected by the Bristol Radical History Group marks the spot.

St Peter's Hospital was destroyed in the 1940 blitz.

Flax Bourton Workhouse. The new, purpose-built, workhouses had a penal flavour about them.

ALL WELCOME - EXCEPT THE ILLEGITIMATE

- Muller's orphanage -

I t is difficult to believe that, not long ago, the suburb of St Andrew's was a place of pilgrimage and small miracles. Visitors to Bristol at the beginning of the 20th century were encouraged not only to visit the great sights of the city, such as the Suspension Bridge and St Mary Redcliffe, but also venture up Ashley Hill to Muller's Orphan Houses. While London had Dr Barnardo (1845-1904), Bristol had George Muller (1805-98).

A guidebook of 1910 states: 'Here, on the top of the hill, healthy and pleasantly situated, are those marvellous instances of answered

Muller, a man of astounding faith, ran his institution on the pledge that 'he would ask for money from no man'.

faith which rebuke the scepticism of the present time, and belong not so much to Bristol as the whole world'.[22]

George Muller founded his orphanage in 1834 in Wilson Street, St Paul's. Condition of entry to Muller's orphanage was straightforward: all were welcome. All were welcome with one exception – the illegitimate. It was a typical Victorian twist; young people, who through no fault of their own were born out of wedlock, were not

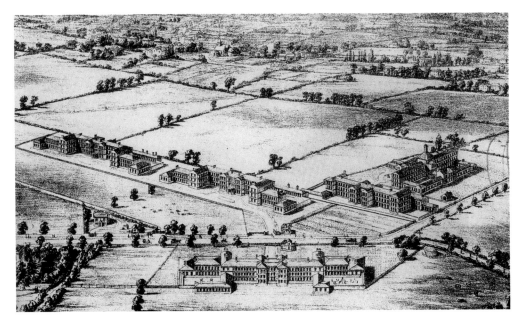

Muller bought seven acres of farmland on Ashley Hill. By 1870 there were five houses accommodating more than 2,050 children.

The houses of the orphanage were a forbidding sight – reminiscent of a workhouse or prison.

offered help.

The demand for places in the Wilson Street home outstripped availability. Another adjacent house in Wilson Street was bought. But this was quickly filled. During the Victorian era the birth rate and survival rate were rocketing. It was clear that something radical had to be done. A purpose-built house was needed.

Muller bought seven acres of farmland, just outside the city boundary, on Ashley Hill, and opened his first house in 1849. By 1870 there were five houses at Ashley Down, costing over £100,000 and housing more than 2,050 children. Over 200 staff were employed – many of them living in.[23]

The houses of the orphanage were an incongruous and forbidding sight – reminiscent of a workhouse or prison – a cluster of enormous grey institutional buildings,

'destitute of ornament', sitting isolated in the countryside. Muller's five orphan houses were all built on a similar plan and were self-contained, having their own laundries and medical facilities. The grounds were used for the cultivation vegetables.

The orphans ranged in age from just a few months up to 17. The girls were trained for service while the boys were apprenticed to a useful trade 'of their choice'.

Muller, a man of astounding faith, ran his institution on the pledge that 'he would ask for money from no man'. Yet the money flowed in – If, at times, somewhat precariously. Apocryphal tales abound. On one occasion, when funds for food had virtually run out, a horse towing a baker's delivery van stopped outside the orphanage and refused to budge. It would only move when all the bread had been unloaded and distributed to the children.

While Muller never asked for money he made sure that there were ample opportunities to make donations. There were daily tours of the orphanage. They lasted one and a half hours and gave an opportunity for the public to see the work and contribute financial support if they felt so moved.[24]

Muller spent his last years living in an austere room in Orphan House Number Three. He died in 1898 at the age of 92 and was buried in Arnos Vale Cemetery. So many people turned out to pay respects to his funeral cortege that the centre of Bristol was brought to a standstill.

The work of the orphanage continued largely unchanged for another 50 years. In all, over 17,000 children were housed between 1849 and 1952.

It was with the beginning of the Welfare State after the Second World War that the care of orphans was re-evaluated. The belief was that it would be far better for parentless children to be looked after by foster parents or cared for in smaller children's houses

As a result of the 1948 Children Act the Muller Trustees decided to sell the five homes at Ashley Down. They bought instead, smaller properties to house family groups of from ten to 12 children. It was felt that this would provide the children with a more natural environment in which to grow. Married couples were taken on as house parents to care for the children and they were helped by assistants.

Eventually, the five Ashley Down houses were purchased by the Local Education Authority in 1958. One is now used by City of Bristol College while the other four have been converted to housing.

From today's perspective, Muller's massive unadorned houses can appear bleak and institutional. They look as if they could crush the spirit of even the most resilient child. But one should not forget that the Muller homes offered a structured upbringing, education and hope when it was needed most. The alternative, in the workhouse, could have been far, far worse.

The Muller Museum, Loft House, Ashley Down Road, BS7 9FG. Interactive, multi-media museum, located in one of the original Orphan Homes, enables visitors to explore what day to day life was like for the orphans. Free entry but you need to book in advance: www.mullers.org/museum

HOUSES, FLATS AND PRE-FABS

- Bristol's Council Housing -

It is only in the last 35 years that home ownership has become the ultimate aspiration. Indeed, until the beginning of the 20th century, it is estimated that 90% of houses were rented from private landlords.[25] The conditions of letting varied. The more well-to-do generally paid their rent quarterly or half yearly – usually Candlemas (2 February) and Michelmas (28 September). The less well-off would pay weekly.

Bristol's first council-funded accommodation was a lodging house, or municipal hostel, built in 1905, in Wade Street, just off Old Market.[26] Aimed at labourers new to, or visiting, the city, the accommodation was one step up from the workhouse.

Over the following ten years there were a number of small scale developments in East Bristol, mostly to house people displaced by slum development and road improvement schemes. Contemptuously referred to as 'brick built barracks'[27] these included basic tenement dwellings in: Fox Road, Easton; Mina Road, St Werburghs; Chapel Street, St Philips; Braggs Lane, Old Market; Millpond Avenue, Easton; and Fishponds Road, The balcony-accessed flats in Mina Road, simple two storey workmen's dwellings, are the only properties to remain from those days.[28]

Meanwhile, Bristol Garden Suburb Ltd was set up in 1909 by Eliza Walker Dunbar (1845-1925) and Elizabeth Sturge (1850-1944). Sturge, a Quaker, had worked as an assistant to the housing reformer and founder of the National Trust, Octavia Hill, in Southwark in the 1880s. The intention for the Bristol Garden suburb was to implement the ideas of Ebenezer

In Shirehampton, houses for 'all classes' were promised in a utopia of 'adequate open spaces' and generously proportioned gardens.

Shirehampton. Only two streets of the planned scheme of 'healthy homes in salubrious surrounds' were completed.

Howard (1850-1928) who had put forward his philosophy of sustainable living in *To-morrow: A Peaceful Path to Real Reform,* published in 1898. A practical man, Howard had bought land, raised money and built two garden cities: Letchworth and Welwyn Garden City.

In Shirehampton, houses for 'all classes' were promised in a utopia of 'adequate open spaces' and generously proportioned gardens.[29] Progress was interrupted in 1914 by the start of the First World War (1914-1918) and only two streets, about one fifth of the planned scheme of 'healthy homes in salubrious surrounds', were completed.[30]

It was at the end of the war that Lloyd George (1863-1945) promised to build 'a country fit for heroes'. This was a new approach reflecting changed times. Following the carnage of the trenches the working population was demanding better conditions. Revolution was in the air; unions were becoming increasingly powerful.

Previously, housing had largely been in the hands of private investors. Now, local councils were compelled to undertake ambitious house building programmes. Four green-field sites were chosen on, or near, the edge of the city. Work began in 1919 at Fishponds (Hillfields); Knowle; Shirehampton and Sea Mills. The first sod was cut at Sea Mills, where an oak tree was planted by the Lady Mayoress to mark the occasion.[31] Hillfields, however, was the first

Bristol's earliest council housing – Mina Road, St Werburghs.

estate to receive residents in 1920.

These houses, with their cottagey, English vernacular feel, were constructed to a high standard and owed much to the influence of Howard. In Knowle Park there were a generous 12 semi-detached houses to an acre.

Bristol's Farms

It is sometimes difficult to believe that much of present day Bristol stands on what were previously agricultural lands supporting dairy herds, nurseries and orchards. Filwood was once a medieval deer park. At Pen Park there was a medieval rabbit warren. Until the 17th century many houses, even in the central parishes of the city, had orchards in their back gardens. A handful of these farm houses still stand, marooned like oases in a desert of housing estates.

Bishopsworth Farms in the 1920s.

Until the 1940s Bishopsworth, in South Bristol, was an agricultural area given over to mixed and dairy farming.

The lost farms of Hartcliffe and Withywood:
- Bishport Farm
- Brook Farm
- Chestnut Farm
- Crox Bottom Farm.
- High Ridge Farm
- Inns Court Farm
- Oakhill Farm
- Pigeonhouse Farm
- Pottery Farm
- Redhouse Farm
- Whitehouse Farm
- Withywood Farm

In 1949 Bristol City Council made a compulsory purchase of much of this farming land for the development of Hartcliffe. Although the farms have long gone the memory of some live on in road and street names.

Hillfields. After the First World War local councils were compelled to undertake ambitious house building programmes.

Roads such as Broad Walk had wide verges and trees. Gardens, bounded by prim privet hedges, were of a good size and each was planted with a fruit tree. Many of the houses had two living rooms and were called 'parlour houses'. The rent was collected weekly, door to door. But with postwar inflation the money to build houses quickly ran out and by July 1921 the building came to a halt.

A second tranche of cheaper and smaller houses (with fixed baths) was built following the Housing Acts of 1923 and 1924. This enabled the first four estates to be completed and new ones started in: Bedminster Down; Horfield; St Anne's Park; St George (Speedwell) and Southmead (started 1931).

Knowle West became the largest estate with 6,000 homes and a population of over 27,000 –the size of a town.[32]

New dwellings were also required for those displaced by inner city slum clearance. Much of the old housing in the city centre was crowded between factories, had no inside sanitation and was cramped, dark and airless. Shoddily built terraced houses, the Victorian solution to the housing crisis, had quickly become slums. In 1923, 112 families were moved from rundown properties in Eugene Street, Kingsdown, to low budget flats at Lawford's Gate, Old Market. To keep the rents as inexpensive as possible, there were no bathrooms.[33] Tenants were expected to use the public baths and wash facilities at Broad Weir. Those displaced by demolition of houses in the Dings were moved to St Anne's.[34] In all, between 1918 and 1939, 15,000 dwellings, housing 65,000 people, were built on the nine main estates that ringed the city.[35]

The fabric of the new buildings might have been better but it wasn't all domestic delight. Some families felt displaced; they missed the intimacy of the crowed inner city housing. The old networks of community life had been lost. It was a half hour tram or bus journey to the city centre; some even said it was too quiet.

The Second World War put an end to further house building for a while. To make matters worse, over 3,000 houses were lost in Bristol and many thousands more badly damaged by bombing.[36] Even before the end of the war ambitious plans were being developed for the reconstruction of the city.

After the war the Labour government pledged 'to house every family on this island'. There was an urgent need for the bombed areas to be reconstructed. By 1946 the waiting list for council housing stood at an unprecedented 26,000.[37]

The 1950s was an era of multi-storey buildings and tower blocks, inspired by modernist architects such as the Swiss born Le Corbusier (1887-1965). In Redcliffe, the first new flats in Canynge House opened in 1954. Canynge House epitomised the arrival of the welfare state and post-war idealism: there was a communal laundry; a crèche; a doctor's surgery and stores for bikes and prams.

At a height of 150 ft, the 15-storey Barton House, Barton Hill, completed in 1958, was the tallest block of flats outside London.[38] Although, these days, tower blocks generally get a bad press, many long-term residents have grown to love them and fear their demolition.

New post-war estates on the far edges of the city included: Henbury; Lawrence Weston;

New post-war estates on the far edges of the city included: Henbury; Lawrence Weston; Stockwood; Hartcliffe and Withywood.

Stockwood; Hartcliffe and Withywood.[39] In addition to housing, there was now an emphasis on the provision of community facilities such as pubs, shops and schools, giving each new suburb a strong sense of identity. But that was only half of it – at Hartcliffe there were also plans for a cinema, a cricket pavilion and a network of youth facilities.[40] But, yet again, money was tight and these were never provided.

Withywood School was opened in 1959; Hartcliffe School in 1960. Employment, though, often necessitated a costly five mile bus journey into town.

'Being on the edge of the city meant that it was only a short walk to the countryside and the estate itself was very green with plenty of open space.'[41] From these idyllic beginnings, there have been times when the urban fringe estates and their residents have felt a little too remote from the workings of the Council House. This was particularly so in Hartcliffe, when the major local employer, Wills, closed their factory.

But why build tower blocks on the edge of the city, where there was less pressure on the land? Simply, because the 1956 Housing Subsidies Act encouraged the construction of high rise buildings by offering a subsidy for blocks of more than six storeys. A flat in a six storey block received 2.3 times the basic subsidy paid on a house. In the end it turned out that tower blocks did not offer higher density housing than low rise because of the space that had to be left around them to avoid problems of shadowing or overlooking.[42]

By 1973, over a third of families in Bristol lived in council accommodation.[43] At its height, in 1981, Bristol City Council owned 47,900 houses and flats. This number dropped quickly as the Thatcher government promoted 'the right to buy' by discounting house sale prices by up to 50%, while also encouraging local authorities to out-source the provision of housing services to independently run housing associations.[44]

Council housing offended the *thatcherite* principles of the *free market*. Without the shelter of state funding, it was argued, the market for housing would become more cost efficient. And for the well-off working class the right to buy was popular.

By 2010, the local authority had 28,435 dwellings in the city, while housing associations administered another 10,744. But the supply of housing was nowhere near meeting the demand. In 2018 it was reported that there were over 11,000 households on the council housing waiting list in Bristol.[45]

There has always been a battle to provide enough healthy and affordable homes. New dwellings are essential for a growing population; replacement homes are required for houses that are old and worn out. The long-standing battle for affordable homes continues.

If you fancy exploring Bristol's housing heritage there is a book of walks around the city's historic housing estates: Homes for Heroes 100, by Melanie Kelly, published Bristol Cultural Development Partnership, 2019.

Bristol's Prefabs

The urgent need for accommodation at the end of the Second World War demanded a radical solution. The answer was the development of the 'prefab': quick-build temporary houses constructed with novel materials such as steel and aluminium.[46] These pre-fabricated homes were assembled in factories, such as the Bristol Aeroplane Company, that had spare capacity once their flat-out wartime production had come to an end. The prefabs were transported in four parts by lorry to where they were needed. A minimal work force was required to assemble them – the parts were placed on a low brick wall and then plugged in!

The first pre-fab was completed in June 1945. Over the next three years a further 2,700 were built on sites across the city.[47] The prefabs were supplied with built-in cupboards, central heating, up-to-date kitchens and even a fridge. The largest prefab site was in south Bristol at Ashton Vale, with around 150 homes, followed by Horfield (north Bristol) with 127 prefabs. The temporary accommodation proved to be unexpectedly durable – and popular. Some of the prefabs, which were expected to last just 10 years, were still in use 60 years later. The last remaining prefabs in Seacole Street, Horfield, were demolished in 2014, though there are a number reconditioned ones still in existence in St George and Speedwell.

'THE SKY ABOVE AND THE ROAD BELOW'

- Leigh Woods tramps village -

Not everybody without a home wants to reside in a hostel or institution. There's always the fear of 'rules'. For the first half of the 20th century 'tramps' were a common sight on the roads. The old workhouses (spikes) were required to offer accommodation to people on the 'tramp' who were ostensibly looking for work. Many of these itinerants had been affected by the world wars, had mental health problems or just couldn't settle.

Those tramping the highways and byways would survive by begging, hand-outs, petty theft and the occasional odd-job. In the 1940s and 50s there was a notorious camp of tramps in Leigh Woods. Some slept under the arches of the Portishead railway line, others built simple huts from driftwood found on the banks of the Avon.[48]

'Toby' lived for 29 years in Leigh Woods until his home-made hut was burnt down.

'... there were ten tramps down there. Most of the men that were in the wood were there because something had gone wrong in their domestic lives... three or four of them lived together in a commune... they all seemed to stick together, they weren't lonely. I like to be alone. Well not altogether. I'm not a recluse. I like to commune with nature. I like the sky above me and the road below me.'[49]

When his hovel was destroyed, it was suggested that 'Toby' register with the Social Security and enjoy the benefits of the Winterbourne Rehabilitation Centre. He reacted with horror.

'Can you imagine me going to the Social Security and acquiescing to subjugation? You couldn't imagine me doing that, it would all be typed up and filed away and you'd get a number. That wouldn't go down well, not for me.'[50]

ENDNOTES

1   Nicholls, J.F. & Taylor, J., *Bristol Past and Present, Volume 2*, 1881, Arrowsmith, p.116.

2   Latimer, J., *The Annals of Bristol in the Nineteenth Century (concluded) 1887-1900*, 1902, George's, p.18-19.

3   Bettey, J.H., *The Landscape of Wessex*, 1980, Moonraker Press, p.79.

4   https://www.visionofbritain.org.uk/unit/10362623/cube/TOT_POP

5   Butcher, E.E., *Bristol Corporation of the Poor 1696-1898*, 1972, Bristol Branch of the Historical Association, p.2.

6   Poole, S. & Rogers, N., *Bristol from Below*, 2017, The Boydell Press, p.66.

7   A thin woollen cloth.

8   Latimer, J., *Annals of Bristol – Seventeenth Century*, 1900, George's, p.481.

9   Seyer, S., *Memoirs Historical and Topographical of Bristol*, 1823, Bristol, p.573.

10   ibid., p.13.

11   Poole, S. & Rogers, N., op. cit., p.35.

12   Latimer, J., *Annals of Bristol – Nineteenth Century*, 1887, W.& F. Morgan, p.186-7.

13   Butcher, E.E., op. cit, p.12.

14   ibid., p.278-9.

15   Oakum picking was the teasing out of fibres from old ropes; 'Money for old rope'. It was hard work. The end product was used for caulking ships.

16   Caldicott, R.L., *The Life and Death of Hannah Wiltshire*, 2017, Bristol Radical History Group, p.25.

17   Latimer, J. *Annals of Bristol – Seventeenth Century*, 1900, George's, p.487.

18   Ralph, E., *Government of Bristol 1373-1973*, 1973, Corporation of Bristol, p.39.

19   ibid., p.52.

20   For a fictional account of working in the Nelson Street dole office see my book 'Where's My Money?' 2008, Tangent Books.

21   Martin, M., *Managing the Poor* in *The Making of Modern Bristol*, ed. Dresser, M. and Ollerenshaw. P., Redcliffe, 1996, p.169.

22   Anon, *How to see Bristol*, 1910, Arrowsmith, p.147-50.

23   Taylor, W.E., *The Bristol Orphan Houses*, 1871, Morgan & Scott, p. 42 -159.

24   Anon., *How to see Bristol*, 1910, Arrowsmith, p.150.

25   Muthesius, S., *The English Terrace House*, 1982, Yale University Press, p.17.

26   Malpass, P. & Walmsley, J., *100 Years of Council Housing in Bristol*, 2005, Faculty of the Built Environment, University of the West of England, p.3.

27   Dresser, M., *People's Housing in Bristol 1870-1939* in *Bristol's Other History*, 1983, Bristol Broadsides, p.148.

28   Malpass, P. & Walmsley, J., op. cit., p.3.

29   Hunt, S., *Yesterday's To-morrow*, 2012, Bristol Radical Pamphleteer Pamphlet, p.14.

30   ibid., p17.

31   In 1981, Sea Mills was designated as a conservation area being 'Bristol's finest example of planned post-WWI municipal housing.'

32   Malpass, P. & Walmsley, J., op. cit., p.4.

33   Dresser, M., op. cit., p.154.

34   Malpass, P. & Walmsley, J., op. cit., p.5.

35   Ralph, E., *Government of Bristol 1373-1973*, 1973, Corporation of Bristol, p.60.

36   ibid., p.55.

37   ibid., p.60.

38   Malpass, P. & Walmsley, J., op. cit., p.8.

39   Ralph, E., op. cit. p.60.

40   Smith, P. in Kelly, M.(ed.), *Homes for Heroes100 - Council Estate Memories*, 2019, Bristol Festival of Ideas, p.9.

41   ibid., p.7.

42   Bougham, J., *Municipal Dreams*, 2018, Verso, p.112.

43   Ralph, E., op. cit., p.60.

44   Bougham, J., op. cit., p.5.

45   https://www.bristolpost.co.uk/news/bristol-news/true-extent-bristols-housing-crisis-1573863

46   Bougham, J., op. cit., p.91-2.

47   Malpass, P. & Walmsley, J., op. cit., p.6.

48   https://www.youtube.com/watch?v=73zb5lHjg2E&feature=youtu.be&t=26, accessed 8 February 2021.

49   Harris, G. *Toby.* 1979. Bristol Broadsides, p.20.

50   ibid., p.23.

THE BLITZ

'BRISTOL'S SPIRIT IS HIGH'

- England at war with Germany -

On Sunday 3 September 1939, the Prime Minster, Neville Chamberlain, announced 'that England is at war with Germany'. Initially, the West Country was not thought to be at risk from bombing.[1] Evacuees were sent from London to Bristol, while the BBC moved several of its departments to Whiteladies Road and other nearby addresses. The number of local BBC employees shot up from 70 to 900.[2]

Even so, with the declaration of war the blackout was enforced. Curtains were to be drawn tight, cars were forbidden to use headlights and street lights were turned off. In spite of these measures Bristol was still easily recognizable from the air in the dark. On a clear night the ribbon of the docks shone like silver under the moon. This didn't stop a total of 78 people stumbling into the Floating Harbour because of the blackout. Fortunately none drowned. [3]

The Nazis turned out to be more determined than had been supposed. Bristol, a major port, home to the Bristol Aeroplane

Rescue worker in a ruined house on St Michael's Hill.
Photo: © Bristol Post.

Company (BAC) and numerous other strategic engineering businesses, was seen as a key target. An aerial photograph taken by the Luftwaffe on 3 September 1939 identified Temple Meads Station as well as strategic bridges, lock gates and gas works.[4]

The first air raid, on 20 June 1940, was not successful. Bombs missed the city by miles, splashing harmlessly into the mud of the Severn near Portishead.[5] Three months later

Despite the valiant work of fire-fighters, the old shopping area of Castle Street and Wine Street was reduced to rubble. Photo: © Bristol Post.

the Luftwaffe returned. 68 Heinkel bombers and 52 Messerschmitt fighter planes flew over Bristol in broad daylight.[6] Their target was the BAC works at Filton. The raid was terrifyingly effective.

One bomb made a direct hit on a crowded shelter. A young BAC employee described returning to work two weeks later: 'I cried because all my workmates had gone and there were strangers in their place.'[7] In all, over 90 people were killed and 150 injured in the June raid on the BAC works. Many houses in Patchway and Filton were also damaged.

There was an outcry. The enemy planes had attacked Bristol unheeded. Why was Bristol so inadequately defended? 504 Squadron was hastily transferred from Hendon in Middlesex to Filton Airfield.[8] The next time BAC was targeted, on 25 September 1940,

RAF Hurricanes were waiting and anti-aircraft guns banged into action.[9] The German planes were dispersed and there were no casualties on the ground.

On the night of Sunday 24 November 1940, a fleet of 134 bombers flew over Bristol. Flares were dropped to pinpoint strategic buildings. This was followed first by incendiaries and then by high explosive bombs which demolished buildings, destroyed roads and shattered water mains and other services. The heart of the old city was the target, though the suburbs of Bedminster, Knowle, St George and Clifton were also hit. In Victoria Street 'flames were hundreds of feet high, the heat was terrific, even the shop window glass was melting'.[10] The roads – paved in some places with tarred wooden blocks – were on fire. The night sky turned blood red. Park Street was ablaze end

To make matters worse it was a ferociously cold winter. The fire-fighter's turntables iced-up and water pipes froze. Photo © Bristol Post.

24 November 1940. Park Street was ablaze end to end. Photo: © Bristol Post.

to end.

The next morning residents viewed the devastation. Despite the valiant work of fire fighters the old shopping area of Castle Street and Wine Street had been reduced to rubble. St Peter's church was a shell, the medieval St Peter's Hospital had burnt to the ground, the landmark half-timbered 17th century Dutch House was nothing more than a charred wooden frame.[11] The Auxiliary Fire Service was completely overwhelmed. Support was sought from surrounding counties and beyond. To make matters even worse the water supply failed due to damage to the mains supply. Water was subsequently pumped from the floating harbour.[12] In just one raid 10,000 homes were damaged.[13] A heavily censored *Evening Post* reported that casualties 'were relatively few.'[14] In contrast, the German News Agency boasted that 'Bristol has been wiped out!'.

Two weeks later the bombers returned. Again the city centre was the target; 156 civilians died, another 149 were seriously injured. And so the raids continued. At night people would seek refuge where they could. Public air raid shelters had been built hastily; some were not fit for purpose and had to be rebuilt.[15] The shelters in St Andrews Park were built on the site of a spring and quickly filled with water. Others had their own home-built *Anderson* shelters in their backyards. Some sought protection in railway tunnels and even Redcliffe Caves.

The Mina Road railway tunnel was a popular spot – over 150 people lined the road on either side sleeping on mattresses and sofas.[16] When a bomb demolished Redcliffe Infants School[17] the crater penetrated to the cavern below. People became twitchy and nervous. To make matters worse it was a ferociously cold winter. On 21 January -13°C. was recorded.[18] The fire-fighter's turntables iced-up and water pipes froze. 'The cold was really numbing, it was debilitating. It pulled you down.'[19]

The government's Mass Observation study, a survey of public morale, was concerned that the spirit of people in Bristol was 'shaky'.

Unexploded Satan bomb being removed from outside 7, Beckington Road, Knowle.

'There is quite open defeatism...there is less laughter and cheerfulness in Bristol than in Southampton or other places...'[20] Bristol Corporation was not keen on such a slur. Not to be outdone it undertook its own survey, concluding that Bristol's 'spirit is high'.[21]

The deadliest blitz was on Sunday 16 March. The warning siren sounded at 8.27pm. The all clear wasn't given until 4.15am. This time the targets were Avonmouth and the city docks. Temple Meads and Lawrence Hill were also badly affected, as were other suburbs. The death toll was the worst yet: 257 killed, 391 badly hurt.[22]

The public shelters were seen as defective and inadequate. In consequence, at night thousands of people would leave the city for the safety of the countryside. Those who couldn't afford to pay for a room slept in churches, village halls, huts, barns and even in the open fields. The evening departure, disparagingly called the *yellow convoy,* 'was

like Piccadilly in the rush hour'.[23] The official advice was to 'stay put'. The authorities were concerned that the 'trekkers' weren't on hand to fire watch and wouldn't be around to put out incendiary bombs. 'Let their blasted houses burn', was the uncharitable response of some.[24]

After a particularly ferocious raid on Good Friday, 11 April 1941, Winston Churchill visited Bristol. He was in the city to award degrees at the University of Bristol but also took the opportunity to go on a walkabout. The previous night 177 aircraft had dropped 193 tonnes of high explosives on the city; 180 people were killed and 382 had been injured.[25] Churchill's stroll through the rubble was carefully stage-managed. This didn't stop people from booing and jeering.[26] (This went unreported at the time.) The citizens of the town in the West had had enough. They were hungry, suffering from disrupted sleep, scared and in mourning. Churchill promised: 'We will give it them back.'

Winston Churchill's stroll through the rubble was carefully stage-managed. Photo: © Bristol Post.

Bristol Rubble in New York

The foundations of Bristol Basin in New York were built using the debris of Bristol homes destroyed during the blitz. The rubble was brought over the Atlantic as ballast for ships. At the time, this was kept secret from the people of Bristol.

'Beneath this East River Drive of the City of New York lies stones, bricks and rubble from the bombed city of Bristol in England...It was not their homes but their valour that kept them free', says a commemoration plaque at Bristol Basin, New York, unveiled June 1942.

The newsreel of the Prime Minister's Bristol visit actually features enthusiastic footage of crowds in Cardiff.[27]

Fortunately, the Good Friday attack was the last full-scale blitz. The nights of tragedy and horror were largely over. Further occasional attacks did occur but they were nothing on the scale of previous raids. The enemy was now concentrating its increasingly stretched resources on other fronts.

During 1940-41 Bristol suffered some of the most concentrated air raids in Britain. It experienced more the 30 bombing attacks with 1,299 civilians killed and 3,305 injured. The saying *Blitz Spirit* has passed into the English language. Over time, memory tends to soften the recollection of events. The frequent but unpredictable bombing so nearly brought the brave and courageous citizens of Bristol to their knees. Respite from the blitz came just in time.

CRASH IN ST ANDREW'S PARK

- The Wellington bomber memorial -

On the evening of 30 April 1941 a Wellington bomber swooped over St Bartholomew's church, brushed a row of trees that lined the top end of Maurice Road and crashed into St Andrew's Park. The plane, which broke in half, was carrying live ammunition which began to explode in the ensuing fire. Brave residents from nearby streets rushed out of their houses to help the injured airmen.[28]

The bomber, from RAF Bassingbourn in Cambridgeshire, had been on a training exercise above Sharpness on the River Severn. On its return journey the plane clipped one, if not two, barrage balloons above east Bristol. Why the plane was flying over Bristol is uncertain – it was twilight and cloud cover was not low.

A slate memorial stone erected to commemorate the crash.

The accident, coming just weeks after the devastating Good Friday Blitz, was hushed-up. There was no mention of the crash in the newspapers and the remains of the broken plane were cleared swiftly away. There was a rumour, perhaps spread by the propaganda machine, that the crew were Polish.

It was miraculous more people weren't hurt. Apart from the crew, just one person on the ground, who was looking after a barrage balloon tethered in the park, was admitted to the Bristol Royal Infirmary with burns.

Full details of the crash only became available 30 years later, in 1971, when the archives were opened to the public.[29] A report revealed that three of the air-crew had been injured while another three died. Regardless of the rumour, all the men were British.

In September 2009, a slate memorial stone was erected in St Andrew's Park to commemorate the crash. The poignant unveiling ceremony, attended by relatives of the aircrew, honoured the lives of those brave men who averted what could have been a much worse disaster.

ENDNOTES

1 Belsey, J and Reid, H., *West at War*, 1990, Redcliffe, Bristol, p.17.
2 ibid., p.19.
3 Reid, H., *Bristol Blitz. The Untold Story*, 1988, Redcliffe, p.12.
4 Winstone, R., *Bristol in the 1940s*, 1961, self-published, p.22.
5 Penny, J., *Bristol at War*, 2002, Breedon Books Publishing Co Ltd, p.44.
6 ibid., p.59.
7 Belsey, J and Reid, H., op. cit., p.35.
8 Penny, J., op. cit., p.62.
9 Winstone, R., op. cit., p.5.
10 Reid, H., op. cit., p.9.
11 Anon, *Bristol Bombed*, 1943, F.G Warne.
12 Penny, J., op. cit., p.76.
13 Belsey, J and Reid, H., op. cit., p.49.
14 ibid., p.50.
15 Harrison,T., *Living through the Blitz*, 2010, Faber & Faber, p. 206.
16 Reid, H., op. cit., p.46.
17 Winstone, R., op. cit., p.84.
18 Horton, B., *West Country Weather Book*, 1995, Barry Horton, p.78.
19 Reid, H., *Bristol Under Siege*, 2005, Redcliffe, p.72.
20 Reid, H., *Bristol Blitz. The Untold Story*, 1988, Redcliffe, p.26.
21 ibid., p.27.
22 Winstone, R., op. cit., p.25.
23 Belsey, J and Reid, H., op. cit., p.71.
24 Penny, J., op. cit., p.121.
25 ibid., p.136.
26 Reid, H., *Bristol Blitz. The Untold Story*, 1988, Redcliffe, p.9.
27 https://www.youtube.com/watch?v=ViALFhVdkwg. Accessed 2/1/2020.
28 http://www.wellingtont2905.co.uk/index.html
29 Public Records Office. Ref AIR 29/642.

BRICKS AND STONES

THE LEAST CELEBRATED MAN-MADE BUILDING MATERIAL

- Bricks -

Brick, mentioned in Genesis in the Bible, is one of the oldest, yet least celebrated man-made building materials. Prior to the arrival of the railways in the 1840s bricks were made from local clay. If possible, the clay would be dug, hand-made and fired on-site. There is a brick kiln shown in Millerd's 1673 map of Bristol.

The first wholly brick building in Bristol was built on Broad Quay in 1698.[1] It was an obvious success as the following year the largely brick built Queen Square was begun. With the memory of the Great Fire of London (1666) still fresh in minds, old-style half-timbered construction was largely abandoned for this new fireproof material. Although few of the original Queen Square houses remain, number 36 (built c.1700) and number 29 (built 1709-11) on the south side of the square are fine examples of Queen Anne brickwork.[2] Though, on the east side of the square, at number 61, the wonky brickwork shows that

61 Queen Square. The dodgy brickwork shows the bricklayers hadn't quite mastered their new skill.

36 Queen Square. A fine example of Queen Anne brickwork.

Cattybrook Bricks

Cattybrook Bricks, in a range of colours – red, yellow, buff and blue – have been widely used throughout Bristol. The Cattybrook brickworks near Lower Almondsbury was established in 1865 by Charles Richardson (1814-96), the engineer of the Bristol and South Wales Union Railway. When constructing the Patchway Tunnel, Richardson noticed the local clay produced high quality bricks. The railway tunnel under the River Severn used 30 million Cattybrook bricks.

The Cattybrook brickworks is still in production and is currently operated by Ibstock Brick Ltd.

the bricklayers hadn't quite mastered their new skill.

Building with bricks was taken to new heights during the second half of the 18th century by the Bristol family of masons and architects, the Patys. When they weren't constructing with Bath stone the Patys built houses with bricks of clean and exquisite quality. These houses included those in King Square (1760), Albermarle Row (1761) in Clifton, Brunswick Square (1784) followed by Berkeley Crescent (1787) at the top of Park Street, and a number of detached residences in Montpelier.[3]

By the second half of the 19th century machine-made bricks had become the favoured building material in Bristol. When Victoria Street (1870s) was constructed between Temple Meads Station and Bristol Bridge it was specified that the buildings were to be fronted with brick.[4] The challenge was accepted with enthusiasm and a novel and exuberant building design emerged that utilised multi-coloured bricks and established a new building style: Bristol Byzantine.

The Granary, Welsh Back. The best example of Bristol Byzantine style using Cattybrook bricks.

A GEOLOGICAL TEXTBOOK

- Stones -

Caen stone was used in the construction of Bristol's oldest building, St James's Priory. c.1160.

Abandoned pennant sandstone quarry by the Frome at Frenchay.

The Bristol region is one of the most geologically varied parts of Britain.[5] The landscape offers a geological textbook of rocks formed by fire, water and wind and provides a rich range of building materials in a variety of textures and colours.

When it comes to stone for building 'the nearer the better' is the maxim. Having said that, the Normans were so partial to their distinctive creamy white Caen stone that they exported it by the shipload all the way from Normandy. This use of alien stone was very much a statement that the Normans were here to stay. The Tower of London was constructed of Caen stone as was Canterbury Cathedral. Locally, Caen stone was used in the building of the castle as well as Bristol's oldest surviving building, the priory church of St James (c.1160).

Until the 17th century, Bristol's domestic buildings were mostly wooden. Although the city avoided a conflagration similar to that experienced by London in 1666, building regulations in the 17th century began to specify the use of less flammable materials.

Bristol's Victorian suburbs get their predominantly grey colour from the unlovely pennant sandstone used in their construction. Pennant sandstone, dug locally, and associated with coal-bearing rocks, is hard but friable. Unlike Bath stone, it is difficult to cut into smooth blocks or sculpt so it is generally used roughly cut. The traditional Bristol paving slab, often heavily grooved, is also Pennant sandstone. Long abandoned Pennant sandstone quarries can be seen alongside the Frome at Frenchay.

For ornamentation around doors, windows and lintels, the easily cut and carved, more attractive oolitic limestone is used. The nearest oolitic limestone quarry was on Dundry Hill. This was the source used by the master masons when they built the Abbey

Dundry Dole Stone in Dundry churchyard. A massive block of locally quarried oolitic limestone.

Fine pale Portland stone, 37-39 Corn Street. Elevation by Sir Giles Gilbert Scott. Relief figure by Hermon Cawthra.

Church of St Augustine (now Bristol Cathedral) and St Mary Redcliffe. It is said that the stone was floated on rafts down the Malago Brook – which must have been a faster running stream in those days. During the 13th century, Dundry stone was in great demand, shipped as far away as Ireland where it was used in the construction of Christ Church Cathedral,

Classic building materials
– where to see them
- Bath Stone – Corn Exchange, Corn Street; Wills Memorial Tower, Park Street
- Brandon Hill Grit – Red Lodge, Park Row.
- Devonian Sandstone (from Monmouthshire) – piers of Bristol Bridge.
- Dundry Stone – St Mary Redcliffe.
- Ham Hill Stone – entrance columns of the old Colston (Beacon) Hall.
- Pennant Sandstone – Arnolfini.
- Slag Bricks from brass smelting – Black Castle, Brislington.

Dublin and St Canice's Cathedral, Kilkenny. Many churches and ecclesiastical buildings in South Wales used Dundry stone; it can also be seen in the walls of Chepstow Castle.

The Dundry quarry ceased as a major supplier in the early 18th century when it became cheaper to bring high quality stone by boat along the canalised Avon (1727) from Bath. The Dundry quarry was last used in the 1920s.

Stone for the rebuilding of Bristol Bridge – opened in 1768 – was floated on trows down the River Wye from Courtfield, near Monmouth.[6]

Brandon Hill Grit is a rough finished reddish tinged stone seen around Clifton. Less frequently used is the greyer and smoother carboniferous limestone which was quarried along the Avon Gorge. Its sharp angular lines made it a favourite for garden rockeries.

Ornamental stone from further afield includes Ham Stone – which has a beautiful golden brown hue but weathers badly – from Somerset and the fine pale Portland stone. This celebrated Dorset stone was used for the building of St Paul's Cathedral in London. Several buildings in Corn Street (nos 31, 37 –

Coping stone made of slag from the brass industry.

Pennant sandstone was used predominantly for Muller's Orphan Houses on Ashley Down. Now residential flats.

39) are faced with it.

And finally, slag from the copper industry[7] was compressed into rectangular blocks and triangular wall copings. These seemingly indestructible, wrinkled black slabs, many dating from the 18th century, were used to construct William Reeve's fairytale Black Castle at Arnos Court. It also randomly crops up in walls across the city.

Recycled building materials

Being green and re-using building materials is nothing new. Work in the 1970s on Numbers 7 and 8 King Street (then the offices of architects Moxley, Jenner and Partners) offered a fascinating insight into 17th century building methods. Parts of the building's timber frame came from a ship; some of the wall laths were recycled barrel staves, while the stone used in the well had originally been ship's ballast brought from afar.

ENDNOTES

1   Evans, J., *A Chronological Outline of the History of Bristol*, 1824, Bristol, p.249.

2   Foyle, A., *Pevesner Architectural Guides - Bristol*, 2004, Yale University Press, p.165.

3   Priest, G., *The Paty Family*, 2003, Redcliffe, p.70.

4   Gomme, A., Jenner, M., & Little, B., *Bristol - an architectural history*, 1979, Lund Humphries, p.336.

5   Stonebridge, E., *Bristol Heritage in Stone*, 1999, Thematic Trails, Oxford Brookes University, p.2.

6   Matthews, W., *Bristol Guide*, 1794 (Facsimile Edition), p.36.

7   Buchanan, R. A., *The Industrial Archaeology of Bristol*, 1967, Bristol Branch of the Historical Association, p.7.

THE BUILDINGS OF BRISTOL

BRISTOL'S BEST NORMAN ARCHITECTURE

- Three Norman buildings to visit -

The soaring Norman castle may have gone (Volume I p.27). There are, however, three other Norman buildings in the Romanesque style – rounded arches and fat columns – that are worth a visit.

Chapter House (c. 1160) of St Augustine's Abbey, now Bristol Cathedral. Entered through an impressive vaulted vestibule, the Chapter House is a riot of Romanesque zig-zaggery. Almost every inch of this rectangular vaulted hall is carved with shallow geometric decoration 'echoing', wrote architectural historian Mike Jenner, 'the dark forest and the cold northern seas of the Norman world'.[1] Fantastically atmospheric.

Between the Cathedral and the Central Library stands what was once the **Gateway to St Augustine's Abbey**. In Tudor times the Romanesque gatehouse was extended upwards. Look out for the Tudor roses. Again the archway displays a marvellous array of chevrons, zig-zags and Celtic knots. To the south of the gatehouse is Abbey House, now part of Bristol Cathedral Choir School, with its

The gateway to what was once St Augustine's Abbey displays a marvellous array of Romanesque chevrons, zig-zags and Celtic knots.

Romanesque 12th century doorway.

In contrast to the Chapter House, **St James Priory** (founded 1134) has a Norman nave which, untypical for the Romanesque style, is elegant and light. Note the distinctive and unusual wheel window (c.1160) in the West front.

THE SOUL OF BRISTOL'S PAST

- *St Mary Redcliffe* -

Look out for the medieval portraits in the stained glass. Is that Thomas à Becket (1118-70) with a bloody cutlass in his head?

St Mary Redcliffe is the soul of the city personified: original, creative, outward looking, adventurous and beautiful.

The north porch's unusual window tracery has been described as being like 'angel's wings.

I f there is one building that captures the soul of Bristol's past, this is it. St Mary Redcliffe was constructed in the 13th and 14th centuries on the site of a former, smaller, church (1190). St Mary Redcliffe stands on a bluff of red sandstone: the red cliff. When it was built it was outside the city gates. The church's most notable feature, the graceful spire, was damaged in a storm in 1446. A new spire, reminiscent of Salisbury cathedral's, was built between 1870-72. It is 89 metres high (292ft).

Inside, the nave is one of the most spectacular in the country. The high roof floats on heavenly clustered pillars of local Dundry stone. The architecture is not wholly English. The unique hexagonal north porch (c.1320[2]) possesses Moorish curves reminiscent of Islamic Spain. The porch's unusual window tracery has been described as being like

St Mary Redcliffe. The high roof floats on heavenly clustered pillars of local Dundry stone.

'angel's wings'.[3]

There are relics of great Bristol lives: a carved, larger than life, unknown medieval knight in chain mail; merchant William Canynges (1402-74) (two tombs!); a simple plaque to Thomas Chatterton (1752-70), the doomed teenage poet; and less romantic, a memorial to Sir Francis Freeling (1764-1836), the founder of the Post Office.

There are scattered mementoes: the bleached rib of a whale apparently returned by explorer John Cabot (1450-1500?); a folksy but evocative wooden statue of Elizabeth I (1558-1603); the bold armour of Samuel Pepys's one-time boss, Sir Admiral William Penn (1621-70) and, in the churchyard, a stone slab engraved 'The Church Cat 1912-1927'.

Enjoy the stained glass. Slithers of original glass have been rescued and reassembled in the north and west windows of the tower. Look out for the lifelike medieval portraits. Is that Thomas à Becket (1118-70) with a bloody cutlass in his head? A modern window of rainbow hue by Harry J. Stammers (1975) gives a dash of colour. It's unusual to see high-heels and a very 20th century handbag featured in a church window.

Take your time and wander around the church. You will be rewarded. St Mary Redcliffe is the soul of the city personified: original, creative, outward looking, adventurous and beautiful.

St Mary Redcliffe. A folksy but evocative wooden statue of Elizabeth I (1558-1603).

A BUILDING TO ENJOY

- *Bristol Central Library* -

Here's a question. What does Bristol Central Library and Southgate Underground Station on the London Piccadilly Line have in common? Answer: they were both designed by Lancashire born architect Charles Holden (1875-1960).

The Bristol Central Library is a building to enjoy. Some say Charles Holden was influenced by the great Scottish architect Charles Rennie Mackintosh (1868-1928), others claim Mackintosh was influenced by Holden. There are striking similarities – especially if viewed from the south – between Mackintosh's Glasgow Art School and the Central Library, both built during the same period. Maybe it's merely synchronicity. In the end, does it matter?

The library, six storeys high, was built on a difficult sloping site. A challenge was to blend the building with the Abbey gatehouse to the east. The north side echoes the gatehouse's round Norman arch and Tudor oriel window. The rear, south side of the building, with its rounded staircase tower and oriel windows, has been described as neo-Tudor.

The city had been left £50,000 by barrister and banking heir, Vincent Stuckey Lean (1820 -99) for the erection of a new Reference Library.[4] Expense wasn't spared and there is much to be admired. The Byzantine inspired entrance hall is welcoming, exotic and surprisingly un-bookish. The walls are lined with a variety of Italian marble, the ceiling covered with gorgeous turquoise vitreous tiles. What a way to enter a library.

The quality of the craftsmanship is superb.

The Byzantine inspired entrance hall of Bristol Central Library is welcoming, exotic and surprisingly un-bookish.

Walk up the curving grand staircase, hold the tactile brass handrail, and admire the stained glass in the oriel window. Before you enter the Exhibition Gallery examine the bronze plaque, 1950, of Holden on your right.

Upstairs the lofty Reference Library reading room, smelling faintly of polish and musty books, with its rows of cubicle tables, also designed by Holden, is the perfect place to write and study.

Through glass doors is The Bristol Room, with its exquisitely carved Grinling Gibbons (1648-1721) fireplace. The Bristol Room is a recreation of the reading room in the original 1740 King Street library.

In 2015 the two lower floors of the Library were controversially acquired by Bristol Cathedral Primary School. While the Newspaper and Magazine Room and storage space were lost, the main library upstairs feels generally unaffected.

Author disclosure: In case you haven't guessed, Bristol Central Library is one of the author's most treasured buildings in Bristol.

THE CHURCH THAT MOVED

- St Werburgh's -

What do you do when a church no longer has any parishioners? Change its use? Knock it down? Or maybe move it to where there is more demand? Which is exactly what happened to St Werburgh's Church.

St Werburgh's Church – founded in 1190 and named after an Anglo Saxon Saint celebrated for restoring a dead goose to life! – was moved from its original position in Corn Street to Mina Road in 1878. This was the second time the church had been rebuilt. The original St Werburgh's had become so decayed that it was taken down, reconstructed and reopened in 1761.[5]

During the Victorian period, as suburbs grew, the old city centre slowly emptied of residents. By the 1870s not one person lived in the tiny parish St Werburgh. It was therefore decided to relocate the church to a more populated area to the east of the city. The contractor, John Bevan, was engaged to reuse the old materials as much as possible – though the new church was larger with some of the original features swapped around.[6] Certainly, the six original bells, one dating back to 1400, were re-hung.[7] Forty large chests of human remains were also removed to Greenbank Cemetery.[8]

Then, 120 years later, the church once again became redundant. This time, rather than transport the building to a more deserving area, it was bought by The Bristol Climbing Centre. The sheer sides of the nave have now been converted to 15m (50ft) high climbing walls. An imaginative and popular solution.

St Werburgh's Church – named after an Anglo Saxon saint celebrated for restoring a dead goose to life!

FORGOTTEN ARTS AND CRAFTS PIONEER

- Edward William Godwin -

Hanging in the Musee D'Orsay, Paris – surely one of the greatest art galleries in the world – is a glass-doored cabinet (1877) that epitomises the Anglo-Japanese movement so popular in the latter part of the 19th century. This piece of furniture is by Bristol-born architect and polymath Edward William Godwin (1833-86).

Godwin was inspired to become an architect by his father, who cluttered the family garden with architectural salvage from old churches.[9] After training in London, Godwin went to work with his brother in Ireland, but after two years returned to England. At the age of 31, in partnership with Henry Crisp (1825-96), he set up his own architectural practice in Bristol.

Like his contemporary, William Morris (1834-96), Godwin designed not only buildings but also furniture, fabrics and wallpaper. He became a friend of the rich and famous, mixing with the likes of Oscar Wilde (1854-1900), the painter James McNeil Whistler (1834-1903) and was romantically linked to the well-known actress Ellen Terry (1847-1928) – who visited him at his home at 21 Portland Square.[10] Godwin relocated to London in 1867 and subsequently eloped with Terry, with whom he had a son. From a professional point of view his move to London proved a mistake; he failed to fulfil his early promise.[11]

While his name is largely forgotten, one of the Bristol buildings Godwin was responsible for is known for all the wrong reasons. For 40 years his robust Carriage Works (1862) on Stokes Croft stood empty and decaying. Now, at last, the site is being redeveloped and the

For over 40 years Edward Godwin's robust Carriage Works (1862) on Stokes Croft stood empty and decaying.

Two gothic brick houses in Stokes Croft (next door to Hamilton House) designed by Edward Godwin. Additional decoration supplied by Banksy.

façade to Godwin's building retained.

One hundred metres away, in Stokes Croft (next door to Hamilton House), are two gothic brick houses. Very different in style from the Carriage Works, they were also designed by Godwin.

Like his Carriage Works, it is about time Godwin's name is rescued from oblivion.

LARGE SCALE TOWN PLANNING

- Bristol's squares -

The concept of a civic square is nothing new. Squares were a central feature of the classical towns and cities of ancient Greece and Rome. But a square solely for residential purposes? That was a novel idea.

Until the 18th century Bristol had largely grown in a piecemeal manner. With the arrival of the square we see early evidence of large scale town planning.

Queen Square is said to be the largest perfect square – i.e. the four sides are equal in length – in Europe. ©Bristol Culture (Bristol Museum & Art Gallery).

- Queen Square -

Queen Square is said to be the largest perfect square – i.e. the four sides are equal in length – in Europe. It was built on what was marshy land and named after Queen Anne who visited the city in 1702. Prior to the beginning of construction, what was known as the Marsh had been a popular spot for an evening promenade. There was an

Erected in 1735, some claim this to be the finest equestrian statue in England. It is ironic that William III died after being thrown from his horse.

Queen Square has adapted well for modern use and should be treasured.

avenue of trees, gravel paths and a bowling green. To the south, beyond the dock-side cranes, were bucolic views of the Addercliffe (Redcliffe), Treen Mill with its duck pond and the Somerset countryside beyond. Millerd's map of 1673 shows sheep grazing on the Marsh. Unfortunately, the Marsh was also subject to fly-tipping.

The buildings around the square were put-up over a period of almost 30 years.[12] There were specifications regarding the height, number of floors and building materials. The fronts were to be made of brick with stone ornamentation. Certainly, no old fashioned half-timbered houses were allowed.

The builders were unaware of, or disregarded, the new fire regulations that had come into force in London in 1709. The London Building Act specified window frames were to be set back from the wall by at least four inches.[13] In Queen Square, sash windows – first used locally in Dyrham Park in 1692[14] – were still being built flush with the building face.

The square was intended as an area for up-market residences. Commercial tenants were not allowed and there was a restriction on noisy or noxious trades. Leases of houses

in the square banned blacksmiths, brewers, candle makers or any tradesmen using fires or making 'ill smells'.[15]

The Lord Mayor's Mansion and the Custom House were on the north side. The square became the home of a number of merchants with involvement in the transatlantic slave trade: Abraham Elton's family lived at No.16; Nathaniel Day at No.29.

In 1705, cross rows of lime trees were planted.[16] In the centre of the square an elegant equestrian statue by Flemish sculptor John Michael Rysbrack (1694-1770) shows William III fancifully dressed as a Roman Emperor. The brass statue was sculpted and cast in London and then shipped by boat to Bristol.[17] Erected in 1735[18], some claim this to be the finest equestrian statue in England. The irony is that William III died after being thrown from his horse. Is that a mole hill that the horse rests its hoof on?

For a few years, Queen Square was THE place to live in Bristol. But this was to change with the development of Clifton and the Hotwell, where crescents, more suited to the hilly topography, became all the rage. The Clifton air was fresher, the views more pleasing and the company more exclusive.

An open space, such as the square, which enables large scale gatherings can have its downside. Previously, the Marsh had been known for its 'riotous assemblies'. Queen Square was a focus for the 1831 reform riots, when many buildings were looted and burnt to the ground. The last of the moneyed inhabitants began to feel nervous living there. By 1861 the professionals had left and the houses were mainly occupied by lodgers.[19]

In the 1930s, this beautiful and much admired square was mutilated by a dual carriageway – part of the inner ring road scheme – running diagonally across it. There were no residents left to object.

Today, only a handful of the original brick houses remain. Thankfully, the offending road was removed in 2000 and the square restored to its previous grandeur. The buildings are almost exclusively utilized for commercial purposes; the tree lined lawns provide tranquillity within the vortex of the city. Despite pressures from misguided traffic engineers and general philistinism Queen Square has adapted well for modern use and should be treasured.

- Some other Bristol Squares -

St James's Square, 1716. Destroyed in 1960s for the construction of the St James Barton roundabout (The Bearpit). ©Bristol Culture (Bristol Museum & Art Gallery).

- **St James's Square**. 1716. Two sides of the square were devastated by the blitz. The remaining buildings were demolished to make way for the construction of the post-war Broadmead development and the nearby St James Barton roundabout (The Bearpit).

- **Dowry Square**, Hotwells. 1720s. A three sided square! The south side was intentionally left open to the sun and views of the river.
- **King Square**. 1755. Few of the original buildings remain. In 1809 it was written: 'the walks are covered with gravel,

and bordered with lime trees; it is kept remarkably clean and neat'.[20]

- **Somerset Square**, The Cathay, Redcliffe. 1756. Destroyed by the blitz.
- **Berkeley Square**, Clifton. 1786. Apart from on the east side of the square, many original buildings remain.
- **Brunswick Square**, St Paul's. More car park than square. The original brick south side was built 1766-71. But it underwent an extensive revamp and is now merely a façade to 1980s offices. The square was initially planted with elms. The neo-classical Congregational chapel on the north side opened in 1835. Next door, the Unitarian Chapel contains a glass etching by Richard Long (b. 1945).
- **Portland Square**, St Paul's. Work started in 1790, but halted three years later with the French Wars. It has its own church, St Paul's, 1794. A statue of George III was pulled down in demonstrations in 1813[21]. Square not completed until 1820.
- **Victoria Square**, Clifton. 1845-55. Not really a square! Three terraces developed at different dates and some detached villas. The gardens contain a Cedar of Lebanon and an old Mulberry tree.
- **Fremantle Square**, Kingsdown. c.1841-2. Built on the site of the Civil War fort, Priors Hill. With community garden.
- **Morley Square**, Horfield, 1888. More rhomboid than square. A rough patch of land surrounded by Victorian Villas. Access for residents only.
- **Market Square**, Hillfields. Early 1920s. Despite its name, there has never been a market here.
- **Melvin Square**, Knowle West. 1930s.

Construction begins in Berkeley Square, Clifton, 1786. South East Corner. Brandon Hill in the background. ©Bristol Culture (Bristol Museum & Art Gallery).

Built at the heart of the estate with roads radiating off. The centrepiece was the Venture Inn which acted as both a pub and neighbourhood social centre.[22] The Venture Inn was demolished in 2006.

- **Gainsborough Square**, Lockleaze. Early 1950s. The hub of Lockleaze estate, a spacious square with shops and community centre.
- **Millennium Square**. 2000. Sits upon a two storey underground car park. There are water features, a giant reflective ball containing a planetarium, sculptures of Cary Grant and Thomas Chatterton, and a monster TV screen that shows mostly football. Welcome to the Millennium.

Portland Square has its own church, St Paul's.

A WINDMILL ON EVERY HILL

- *Windmills* -

A delightful carving of a four sailed post mill can be seen on a medieval misericord in Bristol Cathedral.

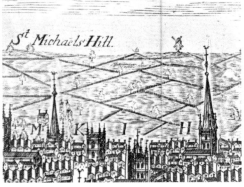

Cotham windmill, first recorded in 1670, can be seen in Nathaniel Buck's 1743 Prospect of Bristol. © Bristol Culture (Bristol Museum & Art Gallery).

The search for sources of free energy is as old as humankind itself. As well as the eponymous Windmill Hill (though nobody is quite sure of the location of the windmill) there were windmills, at one time or another, on Cotham Hill, Brandon Hill, Royal Fort (previously called Windmill Fort) and St Vincent's Rocks.

The earliest windmills would have been post mills, which allowed the windmill to be rotated to catch wind. A delightful carving of a four sailed post mill can be seen on a medieval misericord in Bristol Cathedral.

There is mention in 1565 of a windmill on Brandon Hill[23], while the windmill at Windmill Fort was pulled down in 1643, presumably to make way for the newly built Civil War fortifications.

Later windmills were built with stone towers. With this design, just the cap of the windmill would be turned to move the sails in the desired direction. Cotham windmill, first recorded in 1670, and to be seen in Nathaniel Buck's 1743 *Prospect of Bristol*, was later heightened to become an observatory with splendid panoramic views over Bristol.[24] This tall, slender edifice was demolished in 1953 to make way for school playing fields. A more robust, chess-castle tower is the symbol of Cotham School.

Windmills weren't always on hills. Though, it has to be admitted, the low-lying windmills were the least successful. According to the 1718 edition of Millerd's map, there was a short-lived windmill perched on the red cliff next to Treen Mill Lane (now Guinea Street). Even more surprising were the two windmills for grinding calamine for the Baptist Mills Brass Works in the Frome Valley[25] to the east of the city. One was built around the 1750s, closed in 1814, and finally demolished in the 1830s.[26] The other was capped off and used as a private dwelling until it was knocked down in the 1930s.[27]

In the 18th century Bristol's windmills were mostly used for grinding snuff rather than corn. The Clifton windmill, built in 1766, perched above the Avon Gorge, was badly damaged in a storm in 1777 when, it is said, its sails could not be stopped and the wooden machinery became overheated and self-ignited.[28] This was, apparently, not an uncommon problem for windmills.

Clifton Observatory

The ruin of the burnt-out Clifton windmill was subsequently refurbished and opened as a 'mountain refectory'. Delights such as *Clifton Windmill Biscuits*, milk and Hotwell water were offered for sale to those wishing to enjoy a sublime view of St Vincent's Rock. Closed Sunday afternoons.[29]

Over time further attractions were added. The Clifton Observatory and Camera Obscura was set up in the 1828 by William West (1793?-1861), an artist, who lived with his family in the tower.

The camera obscura is a primitive, yet surprisingly effective, viewing device. It is similar to the optical appliance thought to have been used by artists such Vermeer and Canaletto to capture their remarkably lifelike scenes. The Clifton camera obscura is said to be the only operational camera obscura in England – though there are five others in the UK: in Scotland, Ireland, the Isle of Man and Wales.

A few years later, to extend the attraction, a steep 200ft passage was dug down through the limestone rock to the Giants Cave overlooking the gorge.

LIKE A GALLEON IN A MODERN PORT

- The Dutch House -

The Dutch House stood tightly on the corner of High Street and Wine Street 'like a galleon in a modern port'.

The Dutch House. Its charred frame was so strong it eventually had to be pulled down. (Photo copyright: Bristol Post.)

Sorry, but this building no longer exists. However, the Dutch House is worth remembering as it epitomises the ramshackle nature of the city centre before the blitz. Although destroyed by bombs in the Second World War this black and white multi-gabled house lives on in old pictures of Bristol. It was said to have been constructed in Holland and brought in pieces to Bristol by boat. It stood tightly on the corner of High Street and Wine Street 'like a galleon in a modern port'.[30] During the first half of the 20th century Bristol City Council thought long and hard about its demolition. In 1940 the Council had its mind made up for itself when incendiary bombs did their devastating work. Yet, the venerable building didn't surrender easily.

There are occasional whimsical suggestions that this iconic Bristol building be rebuilt.

A MOST SOPHISTICATED PIECE OF DOMESTIC BUILDING

- Inns Court Farm -

Inns Court Farm, on the edge of Knowle West, dates back to at least the 15th century, maybe even earlier.

For a while the farm was the residence of Sir John Inyn, a Recorder and Chief Justice who died in 1439. While the original farmhouse was knocked down and replaced in the 18th century part of the late medieval building, an ornate two storey porch and stair tower built in Dundry stone, miraculously remains.

The polygonal tower of Inns Court Farm is an important fragment of the building. It has been described as 'a most sophisticated piece of domestic building from the early 15th century.' [31]

In its latter years the porch has had an ignominious history. In the 1930s it was used as a hen house. The farmhouse was then briefly rescued and housed a temporary mission church and vicarage while the Knowle West estate was being built. Today, this important building, one of the few tangible links with South Bristol's past, is dilapidated, boarded-up and surrounded by razor wire.

The tower is now officially listed by Bristol

Inns Court Farm. In its latter years the porch has had an ignominious history. In the 1930s it was used as a hen house.

City Council as a building at risk. English Heritage describes it as being in 'slow decay'. Unless something is done swiftly one wonders how long this neglected building can survive.

A FASCINATING DEPICTION OF SEVENTEENTH CENTURY BRISTOL

- Millerd's map (1673) -

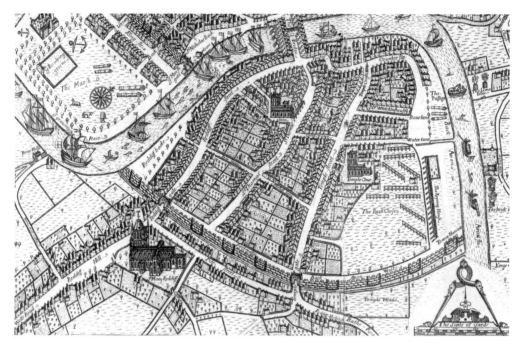

Millerd's Map 1673 (detail). **A fascinating picture of seventeenth century Bristol.** © Bristol Culture (Bristol Museum & Art Gallery).

Bristol is fortunate to have been relatively well mapped over the last 500 years.[32] The earliest map is Ricart's impressionistic plan of 1479 which focuses on the High Cross and the four streets leading to it.

The first recognisably detailed plan of Bristol is William Smith's diminutive print of 1568. Roughly A5[33] in size, this colourful map is the first to identify Bristol's main streets, walls, castle, churches and other prominent buildings.[34] Thirteen years later, a larger plan of Bristol was produced by George Hoefnagel (1542-1610), a resident of Antwerp. Hoefnagel's

plan, which bears striking stylistic similarities to Smith's map, gives a fascinating bird's-eye view from a southern perspective. The impression is of a fortified town in a rural setting. The walls separate the city from the countryside; sheep graze in the surrounding fields while a group of finely dressed Elizabethan figures look on. Meanwhile, the quays are curiously empty of ships and related bustle – perhaps this is what gives the city such a bucolic feel.

But the map that really brings 17th century Bristol alive is the charming Millerd's map of 1673. Millerd describes his plan as:

An exact delineation of the famous citty

of Bristoll and suburbs thereof, together with all the highways, through-fares, streets, lanes and public passages, therein contained...

James Jacobus Millerd was a Bristolian.[35] Over the years, four versions of his Bristol map were produced.[36] In 1686, he published a map of Chepstow; otherwise, little is known of Millerd.

The Bristol map shows a compact but busy port and market town (population 20,000) – hardly the self-proclaimed second city of the Kingdom. You could have walked in any direction from the High Cross to open country in 15 minutes. There are 18 churches and one cathedral. In addition to the ships lined along the Key and the Backs, there are markets, a brick kiln, a lime kiln, racks for drying woollen cloth and a rope walk.

There are two bowling greens, while Brandon Hill is set aside '...for ye use of drying cloths'.

The southern Portwall, with its bastions, is clearly delineated. While Millerd mostly draws stylised domestic buildings – small square houses with sloping roofs – some of the principal buildings are rendered in greater detail. In the more spacious Redcliffe and Temple parishes there are neat vegetable gardens and orchards. Of course, the slums and stinking middens don't feature, though there is the rather telling Dung Wharf. There are delightful vignettes of duck hunts, a horse on a ferry and ships under full sail (unlikely within the confines of the port). And there's a discreet note at the top of St Michael's Hill that apparently warns, if my schoolboy Latin is correct, travellers on the road to Aust Ferry to beware of thieves and prostitutes.

Around the edge of the map are spidery illustrations of Bristol's notable buildings: the Great House on Redcliffe Street; the Custom House and the Guild Hall. Bristol Bridge, with its staggering six storey shops, also features.

Although it may not be, as promised, an 'exact 'delineation', if you want to get a feel for Bristol in the 17th century there is no better way than to study Millerd's map.

Millerd's Map, along with other intriguing cartographic images, can be viewed in Bristol Museum and Art Gallery.

ENDNOTES

1 Jenner, M., *Bristol's 100 Best Buildings*, 2010, Redcliffe, p.13.
2 Smith, M. Q., *St Mary Redcliffe – an architectural history*, 1995, Redcliffe, p.39.
3 Jenkins, S. *England's Thousand Best Churches, 1999*, Allen Lane, p. 233.
4 Beeson, A., *Bristol Central Library and Charles Holden*. 2006, Redcliffe.
5 Shiercliff, E., *The Bristol and Hotwell Guide*, 1809, p.52.
6 Gomme, A., & Jenner, M., op. cit., p.405.
7 https://bristolbells.weebly.com/baptist-mills.html . Accessed 03/11/2020.
8 Latimer, J., *Annals of Bristol in the Nineteenth Century*, 1887, W. & F. Morgan, p.461.
9 Gomme, A., Jenner, M., & Little, B., op. cit., p.435.
10 ibid., p.284.
11 Whittingham, S., *The greatest aesthete of them all*, in *Bristol Review of Books*, issue number 3, 14-6.
12 Evans, J., op. cit., p.260.
13 Yorke, T., *Georgian and Regency Houses Explained*, Countryside Books, p.43.
14 Hall, L., *Period House Fixtures and Fittings 1300 -1900*, 2007, Countryside Books. p.76.
15 Kelly, A. *Queen Square Bristol*, 2003, Redcliffe, p.13.
16 Evans, J., op. cit., p.357.
17 Merritt, D. & Greenacre, F., *Public Sculpture of Bristol*, 2010, Liverpool University Press, p.174-5.
18 Evans, J., op. cit., p.263.
19 Kelly, A., op. cit., p.13.
20 Shiercliff, E., *The Bristol and Hotwell Guide*, 1809, p.85.
21 The statue of Colston was not the first to be pulled down by an angry crowd.
22 Kelly, M. *Homes for Heroes 100 - Book of Walks*, 2019, Bristol Cultural Development Partnership, p.76.
23 Evans, J., op. cit., p.148.
24 Matthews, W., op. cit., p.111.
25 Drawing by S.H. Grimm, British Library Collection.
26 Know Your Place: https://maps.bristol.gov.uk/kyp/?edition=bristol&layer=Community%20layer&x=360128.88&y=174333.36&extent=688.18 26/05/2020.
27 I am indebted to Jill Larke for information about the Pennywell Road windmill.
28 Latimer, J., op. cit., p.430.
29 Evans, J., op. cit. p.285.
30 Morton, M.V., *In Search of England*, 1929, Methuen and Co, p.124.
31 Gomme, A, Jenner, M. and Little, B: *Bristol, An Architectural History: Bristol*, 1979, Lund Humphries, p. 72.
32 Bishop, J., *Bristol through Maps*, 2016, Redcliffe.
33 By today's measurement.
34 Pritchard, J.E., *Old Plans and Views of Bristol*, 1926, Transactions of the Bristol and Gloucestershire Archaeological Society, Vol. 48, p.327-8.
35 Bishop, J., op. cit., p.35.
36 Pritchard, J.E., *A hitherto unknown Original Print of the Great Plan of Bristol by Jacobus Millerd, 1673*, 1922, Transactions of the Bristol and Gloucestershire Archaeological Society, Vol. 44, p.205-6.

THE GRAND HOUSES OF BRISTOL

GRAND HOUSES SET IN PARKLAND

By the end of the 18th century Bristol was ringed by a number of grand houses owned by the city's merchants. Set in landscaped parks, they were an easy coach ride to the city. Yet they were far enough away from the persistent buzz and commotion of the port and its industries to offer an idyllic escape.

Be aware that the spoils of the slave trade, in one way or another, are stamped all over 18th century Bristol – none more so than on its great houses.

- Ashton Court -

There has been a manor house here since the 13th century. The current mansion sits in 830 acres of softly sloping parkland. The house overlooks Bristol as well as having extensive views of the rolling hills to Bath. Directly across the valley is the hilltop village of Dundry with its landmark church tower. The deer park, formed in 1392, is reputed to be one of the oldest in the country.[1]

The Ashton Court Estate came into the hands of John Smyth, merchant, landowner and former sheriff and mayor of Bristol, in 1545. The estate stayed with the Smyths for 400 years – the last Smyth to live here died in 1946.

Ashton Court. The crumbling mansion and surrounding estate was purchased by Bristol City Council in 1959 for £103,000.

In the grounds, hidden among the undergrowth, is an ice house. Ice shipped from Norway in the winter was stored in this dark pit for use throughout the year.

Grand staircase, Ashton Court Mansion. The future of the mansion is uncertain.

In 1802, the celebrated landscape architect Humphrey Repton (1752-1818) advised on scenic improvements to the park. Whether the Smyths acted on his advice is uncertain.

The Smyths owned much land in south Bristol and beyond. They struck lucky in the 19th century when it was found that their estate contained rich coal seams.

Although most of the present mansion is of 19th century construction the building is wrapped around a much earlier core. [2] At its heart is a 14th/15th century great hall. And that may well sit upon prior foundations

The west end of the commanding south front, which overlooks the lawn, was built in the 17th century. To the east of the central tower the building is of early 19th century construction.

The stables, with their fine cast iron stalls, once housed the horses and carriages of the Lord Mayor of Bristol. It is now a tea room.

Taken as a whole, reflecting its hotch-potch development, Ashton Court Mansion is unbalanced and disorientating. 'I have never been able to love it,' wrote the architect and historian, Mike Jenner. [3]

In the grounds, hidden among the undergrowth, is an ice house. Ice was shipped from Norway in the winter and stored in this dark pit for use throughout the year. There is also a cemetery for the Smyth's much loved pets.

The crumbling mansion and surrounding estate was purchased by Bristol City Council in 1959 for £103,000.

The future of the mansion is uncertain. The city council can no longer afford to support the building so alternative income generating uses are being discussed.

There is also a cemetery for the Smyth's much loved pets.

One of oldest trees in Bristol?

The 700-year-old Domesday Oak (nothing to do with the Domesday Book), on a slope above the mansion, is said to be one of oldest trees in Bristol. Although still very much alive, this noble tree is a shadow of its former glory. In the 2010s it was held together by wooden supports and wires. Much of the main body of the oak has since collapsed. Hidden by brambles it is slowly rotting away.

The 700-year-old Domesday Oak (right of picture).

Fifty metres down the hill there are a number of gnarled oaks with even greater girth. According to the Bristol Tree Forum there are over 100 ancient pollarded oaks on the Ashton Court Estate.

The honour of being the oldest tree goes to a female yew in Holy Trinity churchyard, Abbot's Leigh. This venerable tree, seven metres in circumference, is said to be 1,000-years-old, if not more.[4]

- Arnos Court -

'*I was struck by a large gothic building, coal black, and striped with white; I took it to be the devils cathedral. When I came nearer, I found it was a uniform castle, lately built and serving for stables and offices to a smart false-Gothic house on the other side of the road.*'[5]

So wrote Horace Walpole in 1766. With his Strawberry Hill residence in Twickenham, Walpole was the current arbiter of good taste. Unfortunately, he found William Reeve's new mansion rather old-style. When it comes to architecture Bristol was frequently behind the London fashions.

Arnos Court is one of the few Bristol grand houses not perched on a hill – and subsequently is often overlooked. Even in its early days the setting was not ideal. The turnpike road to Keynsham and Bath cut through the estate

Arnos Court. Even in its early days the setting was not ideal.

leaving the stables stranded on the opposite side of the road from the main house.

William Reeve, who built the Arnos Court complex, was a wealthy Quaker with investments in the slave trade. A pugnacious

William Reeve constructed his *Devils Cathedral* with pre-cast copper slag blocks from his brass works. The castle, a sizable building in its own right, housed stables, offices and rooms for entertainment.

The colonnade from Arnos Court was rescued by the eccentric architect Clough Williams-Ellis. It now sits centre-stage in the fairy-tale Italianate village, Portmeirion. Photo: H. Arundale.

character, he also owned the Crew's Hole Copper Works. He once challenged a barrister who had publically ridiculed him to a duel with swords, pistols or fists. 'Thou might'st think, perhaps, that a Quaker might be insulted with impunity,' Reeve said, 'but I am a man of spirit.' The astounded barrister duly apologised.[6]

The quietly elegant Arnos Court house is thought to be the product of another James Bridges (born c.1725) and Thomas Paty (c.1713-89) partnership. But it's the outbuildings that make Arnos Court so interesting.

Over the road from the house, Reeve constructed his *Devils Cathedral* with pre-cast copper slag blocks from his brass works. The black castle, a sizable building in its own right, housed stables, offices and rooms for entertainment. Some think it is the best of all fake castles in Britain.[7] It is now used as a pub.

The castle was originally entered via a forecourt through a 'triumphal' gothic archway – another design by James Bridges. In 1766, Reeve bought the rather unsophisticated medieval sculptures from the recently demolished Lawford's Gate and Newgate to fill the niches.[8] (The current figures are replicas: the originals are on display at M Shed.). The

archway was moved to its present position in 1912 and now stands forlorn and neglected by Junction Road traffic lights.

By far the best of the Arnos Court outbuildings was an ornate stone colonnade that fronted a bath house. A day spent at the brass works, even in the office, was dirty business. A bath on return home was a welcome luxury. And as befits the best of gothic buildings, a secret tunnel ran from the bath house, under the road to the main house.[9]

When the roads were widened, yet again, in 1957, the colonnade was rescued from being broken up by the eccentric architect Clough Williams-Ellis. It was transported to North Wales, where it now sits centre-stage in the fairy-tale Italianate village, Portmeirion.

Reeve's rise to riches was quickly over. He was declared bankrupt during the difficult year of 1774 when trading with North America was disrupted.[10].

In the 1850s Arnos Court was extended at the rear and converted to a convent for the Sisterhood of the Asylum for the Good Shepherd. The house is currently Arnos Manor Hotel.

- The Dower House -

The Dower House is the canary coloured mansion, perched on a ridge, on the north side of the M32. The original house was built by Richard Berkeley in 1553. The current building, designed by Thomas Wright (1711-86), dates from c.1760.

The house passed, due to marriage connections, to the Dukes of Beaufort in 1770 and was then used as a dower house. A dower house is a residence built for the widow of the previous owner of the estate. In this case, it was placed at a discrete distance from the family seat at Badminton, Gloucestershire. It remained in the ownership of the Beaufort family until 1907.

The Dower House stood at the centre of the Stoke Park Estate. Just imagine what it was like before the motorway cut through! The sweeping park, also landscaped by Thomas Wright, included a number of follies, obelisks, tunnels and ponds, some of which remain today. The Duchess Pond was lost under the motorway but was later reinstated as a fishing lake in a slightly different position.

Much of the Stoke Park Estate remains, though chunks have been carved off for the

The Dower House stood at the centre of the Stoke Park Estate. Just imagine what the park was like before the motorway cut through!

Lockleaze Housing Estate (1950s), University of the West of England (1970s) and the Ministry of Defence Abbey Wood complex (1980s) and, of course, the M32 (1960s).

Before it was converted into private apartments in the 1990s, the Dower House was part of the Stoke Park Colony (1909-2000), the largest group of hospitals in the UK for those with learning difficulties. The park is now owed by Bristol City Council.

- Kings Weston House -

Blenheim Palace, Castle Howard and… Kings Weston House. All buildings designed by celebrated 18th century architect and playwright Sir John Vanbrugh (1664 -1726). Vanbrugh specialised in palaces and mega-mansions. While admittedly grand and impressive, Kings Weston House is no palace.

Kings Weston House sits on a bluff with a panoramic view of the Severn and South Wales beyond: a splendid location to watch the coming and going of Bristol's ships. Once 'one of the great views of England' it now looks over an industrial sprawl of warehouses, depots and the M5.

The house was commissioned by Edward

Kings Weston House. Its most notable feature is its inter-connected arcaded chimneys

The high ceilinged entrance salon, with its creamy painted panelling and its black and white stone floor, is impressive and hospitable. From here a door leads to a dark, three storey hall, with an *Escheresque* hanging staircase. None of the other rooms, which have mostly been stripped of their original features, quite live-up to this imposing welcome.

In the middle of the 20th century the house was used as a school of architecture and then a police training college. From 1995 it stood empty and unappreciated until it was privately purchased in 2000. Since then the building has slowly and respectfully been brought back to life.

Southwell (1671-1730), one time Secretary of State for Ireland. It was built between 1710 and 1719 on the site of a previous Tudor mansion. The stone, which weathers in places to a pinkish tinge, was quarried on site. The house is a simple cube, with baroque ornamentation. Its most notable feature being its inter-connected arcaded chimneys. (A feature copied in Bishopsworth Manor, Bishopsworth.) Before the chimneys were constructed, Vanburgh built a life-size mock-up in wood to check how they looked.[11]

It was during a lull in a weekend house party at Kings Weston House in 1914 that the composer Ralph Vaughan Williams (1872-1958) completed his ethereal *The Lark Ascending*. After the hiatus of the First World War *The Lark Ascending* was premiered in 1920 at Shirehampton Public Hall.

- *Blaise Castle House* -

In 1766, Bristol merchant and slave trader Thomas Farr built a sham tower, in the centre of what was once an Iron Age hill fort and is now called Castle Hill. From this eccentric gothic folly, Farr, who owned sugar plantations in North America, could enjoy views out to the Bristol Channel and across to Wales.

Blaise Castle is mentioned fleetingly in Jane Austen's novel Northanger Abbey.

'Blaize Castle!' cried Catherine: 'what is that?'

'The finest place in England – worth going fifty miles at any time to see.'

'What! Is it really a castle, an old castle?'

'The oldest in the kingdom.'

Fortunately, the protagonists never got to see this fine castle; they may have been deeply disappointed.

Farr went bankrupt in 1778 as his businesses faltered during the American Revolutionary

Blaise Castle House. Imposing, but without excessive ornamentation, the mansion reflected J. S. Harford's Quaker beliefs.

In 1766, Bristol merchant and slave trader Thomas Farr built a sham tower, in the centre of what was once an Iron Age hill fort.

War (1775-83).[12] Eventually, the Blaise Estate was purchased by Quaker banker and slave trade abolitionist, John Scandrett Harford (d.1815). Harford demolished the original house and commissioned William Paty (1757-1800) to build a mansion of 'substance, directness, dignity and security.'[13] Constructed 1795-96,[14] a solid and simple Bath stone box is exactly what Harford got. Imposing, but without excessive ornamentation, the mansion reflected Harford's Quaker beliefs.[15]

The conservatory and rustic dairy were added in 1804-6. The mansion's simplicity was tempered somewhat by the later addition of Charles Cockerell's porticoed Picture Room (1832-3).

The landscaping of the estate was executed by Humphry Repton who achieved a number of picturesque vistas mainly by cutting down trees. The natural terrain bordering Hazel Brook was already deemed dramatic enough, so little heavy earth moving was required. Repton was famous for his 'red book' – on show at the Blaise Castle House museum – whereby you flipped the pages to show the 'before' and 'after' effect of his work.

But the real fun begins down the road where Harford commissioned John Nash (1752-1835) to build a rustic hamlet for his retired workers.

The Blaise Castle Estate was owned by the Harfords until 1926, when it was purchased by Bristol City Council.

Blaise Castle House is now run as a museum

If you wander through Blaise Castle Estate down to Hazel Brook you will see Stratford Mill, an 18th century mill house. This stone building originally came from the Chew Valley. It was moved to its present position when the Chew Valley Reservoir was created in the 1950s.

This 18th century mill was moved to its present position when the Chew Valley Reservoir was created in the 1950s.

- Blaise Hamlet -

A fantasy rural idyll

The wonderfully hobbitesque Blaise Hamlet was built in the early 1800s. It was designed by John Nash who was responsible for much of the layout of Regency London, including the remodelling of Buckingham Palace and the design of Regent Street and Regent's Park.[16]

In contrast to these grand designs the nine houses, with cottage gardens, clustered around a village green with its own sundial and water pump, recreated a quaint, romantic idyll that never existed. The interiors were compact but well arranged, each cottage having an oven and a boiler. Some of the houses have pigeon lofts; all have outside benches for the inhabitants to sit and listen to the chatter of jackdaws and enjoy the tranquillity of their gardens. Residents lived rent free, but were expected to maintain their cottages and be on show in their pensioner's uniform for tourists.

Blaise Hamlet is managed by the National Trust. There is free access to the green during daylight hours, but not to the houses.

Residents lived rent free, but were expected to maintain their cottages and be on show in their pensioner's uniforms.

The wonderfully hobbitesque Blaise Hamlet was built in the early 1800s.

- *The Royal Fort* -

Not a fort at all, but a quietly impressive Georgian house tucked away on the University of Bristol campus. It is so called as it was from here that the Royalists established their fortress (1644) during the English Civil War.

In 1758, Thomas Tyndall (1722-1794) bought the lease of a semi derelict house in the Royal Fort, which he subsequently demolished.[17] Tyndall set about building a mansion in a muted rococo style. The house is thought to be designed by the architect James Bridges and constructed by Bristol master masons, the Patys.[18]

James Bridge's origins are uncertain: some say he was American, others that he was the son of a Herefordshire clock maker. One thing we can be certain of, is that he was not a native of Bristol. For a brief period in the middle of the 1760s he grabbed all the major local building contracts (rightly so): the construction of the new Bridge, the remodelling of St Werburgh's Church and the building of Arnos Court. Local builders were envious of this outsider's successes and made life difficult for him. James Bridges disappeared from the city

Royal Fort House was completed in 1761. Thomas Tyndall also acquired several of the surrounding fields and set about converting the meadows into a park. © Bristol Culture (Bristol Museum & Art Gallery).

in 1763, rumoured to be heading for the rich pickings of the West Indies.[19]

Royal Fort House was finished in 1761. Inside, the house is spacious and uncommonly light. With its naturalistic wooden carvings and gorgeous Chinese inspired plasterwork by Thomas Stocking the interior is certainly worth a visit.

Thomas Tyndall also acquired several of the surrounding fields and set about converting the meadows into a park. Tyndall, like his father, was a banker working at The Old Bank in Corn Street.[20] A self-interested man, he was reluctant to serve as a councillor when requested[21] and campaigned against the new Infirmary being set up too close to his secluded park.[22]

In 1792, for unexplained reasons – perhaps it was the £40,000 sale price – Tyndall sold the 48 acre estate to a consortium of speculators who planned to use the land to build a grand terrace and several large houses with splendid views over the city.[23] But with the outbreak of war with France in 1793, and an ensuing financial panic, the scheme stalled. Tyndall died soon after in 1794. The land was subsequently repurchased by Thomas Tyndall's son, also

The Royal Fort. Not a fort at all, but an imposing Georgian house tucked away on what is now the University of Bristol campus.

Thomas (1764-1804) in 1798.[24] Landscape architect Humphry Repton, who had worked at Blaise Castle, was employed to repair the scars inflicted on the terrain by the builders when laying foundations for the ill-fated plan.

The end of the Tyndall's Park Estate came in 1861, when a new thoroughfare, Tyndalls Park Road, running between Whiteladies Road and Cotham Road, was cut across the park. The Tyndalls continued to live in the Royal Fort until 1916 when the house and surrounding land was sold to the University.

ENDNOTES

1   Vear, L., *South of the Avon*, 1978, self-published, Wotton-Under-Edge, p.11.
2   Foyle, A., *Pevesner Architectural Guides - Bristol, 2004*, Yale University Press, p.285.
3   Jenner, M., op. cit. p.30.
4   Drake, F. and D'Arpino, T., *Trees of Bristol*, Redcliffe Press, 2014, p.72.
5   Bettey, J.H., *Bristol Observed*, 1986, Redcliffe Press, p.77.
6   Latimer, J., *Annals of Bristol in the Eighteenth Century*, 1893, Bristol, p.285.
7   Gomme A, Jenner M and Little B., op. cit., p.170.
8   Latimer, J., *Annals of Bristol in the Eighteenth Century*, 1893, Bristol, p.377.
9   https://historicengland.org.uk/listing/the-list/list-entry/1201988. 01/06/2020.
10 Latimer, J., op. cit., p.286.
11 Jenkins, S., *England's Thousand Best Houses*, 2004, Penguin, p. 686.
12 Latimer, J., op. cit., p.435.
13 Jenkins, S., *op. cit.*, p. 684.
14 Foyle, A., op. cit., p.288.
15 Priest, G., op. cit., p.120.
16 Gomme, A., Jenner, M., & Little, B., op. cit., p.284.
17 Latimer, J., op. cit., p.334.
18 Ison, W., *The Georgian Buildings of Bristol*, 1952, Faber & Faber, p.190-1.
19 Gomme, A., & Jenner, M. *An Architectural History of Bristol*, 2011, Oblong, p.410
20 Ollerenshaw, P., *The Development of Banking in the Bristol Region, 1750-1914*, in *Studies in the Business History of Bristol*,1988, ed. Harvey, C. & Press, J., Bristol Academic Press, p.57.
21 Latimer, J., *Annals of Bristol in the Eighteenth Century*, 1893, Bristol, p.219.
22 ibid., p.479.
23 Latimer, J., op. cit., p.494.
24 There is confusion about Thomas Tyndall's date of death. John Latimer writes that Tyndall died in 1790. The register at Christchurch indicates he was buried on 24 April, 1794, his will was certified on 1 May 1794.

CONCRETE
AND CARS

The cars goes by like thunder,
and up and round and under,
just where they goes
nobody knows,
taint no bleedin wonder –

Adge Cutler
Virtue et Industrial

STAIRWAY TO THE FUTURE

- A futuristic plan for Bristol -

Not so long ago there was a concrete stairway on Rupert Street that led nowhere. This folly was a reminder of a futuristic plan for Bristol that was never fully realised. The steps were part of a bold vision that included building aerial walkways that would allow safe passage on foot to shops, offices and civic amenities away from the roaring traffic below. In theory a good idea, but other aspects of the 1960s scheme – the demolition of historic buildings and the construction of urban expressways ripping through the old city centre of Bristol – were

An urban expressway was to cut through historic Queen Square, and cross the docks by Bush House (now the Arnolfini).

less appealing.

Even before the end of the Second World War plans were being considered as to how to reshape Bristol. It was generally agreed that the organic and unplanned development of the centre of the city over the centuries had led to 'an unhealthy crowding together of factories and houses, with no space for gardens, parks and playgrounds'. The town planner, Patrick Abercrombie, who had worked on the 1930 Bristol & Bath Regional Plan, gleefully wrote that the destruction of city centres by war time bombing provided an opportunity 'rarely occurring in modern existence, to re-plan and rebuild a Centre of really modern design'.[1]

One solution, put forward in 1944, was to build a new look Bristol in self-contained neighbourhoods, each with its own shopping centre, clinic, schools, churches, cinema and recreation ground.[2] The Southmead Estate in North Bristol, constructed ten years before, was developed on this model. In the days before universal car ownership such neighbourhoods were considered viable.

Broadmead Shopping Centre

Far-reaching and ambitious redevelopment plans had already been drawn up before the end of the Second World War.[3] After the War there were plenty of opportunities to reshape the heart of the city centre. The first plan, published in 1952, suggested re-siting the shopping centre from the bombed out Castle Street area – now Castle Park – to Broadmead.[4]

This was a great opportunity. Compared with the ancient shops of Castle Street, Broadmead's modern stores were to be brighter, cleaner and more accessible. The emphasis was on replanning rather than rebuilding. They represented an exciting and optimistic future. There was bold talk of a new civic centre on Wine Street, pedestrian areas, futuristic multi-storey car parks, rear access service areas to the shops and improved roads.

Unfortunately, the original plan by the city architect John Nelson Meredith was only implemented in a piecemeal manner.

Apart from a couple of flagship stores, the architecture has been described as 'dowdy and feeble'.[5]

As a memorial to war-torn times the churches of St Peter's and St Mary le Port were left as burnt-out shells. For many years they sat forlornly surrounded by a car park – later to be turned into Castle Park.

As shopping became a 'lifestyle experience' Broadmead underwent several upgrades. In the 1980s the streets were pedestrianised. While, in 1987-90, the Galleries, a three storey indoor shopping mall, was built on the South West quarter of Broadmead. Yet, with competition from the out-of-town Mall at Cribbs Causeway (opened 1998) and the adjoining Cabot Circus (opened 2008) Broadmead has struggled to maintain its popularity as a shopping destination. With the closure of Marks and Spencer in 2022 the future of Broadmead looks uncertain.

Not so long ago there was a concrete stairway on
Rupert Street that led nowhere.

Underpasses, overpasses and elevated walkways
became an integral feature of the new urban
landscape. This is how Redcliffe could have looked.

By the 1960s an updated plan was required to
take into account burgeoning car ownership. In
1951 only 14 per cent of households had access
to a car; by 1971 the figure was 45.per cent.[6]

Although the M4 didn't reach the outskirts
of Bristol until 1972, the opening of the M1 in
1959 had signalled the start of the motorway
age and the dominance of the car in the
urban landscape. As Dr Beeching was axing
the railways, new motorways sprang up in
their place. Deliveries could be made door
to door. The opening of the Severn Bridge
in 1966 (actually two bridges: one over the
Severn, the other over the Wye) cut the road
distance between Bristol and Cardiff by 55
miles. It was a time when cars were king. The
booming middle classes took to the road. (It
became every driver's ambition to do a 'ton'
(100mph) on the M1; the 70mph speed limit
was only introduced in 1965.) From now on
town planning was viewed through the car
window.

The urban planning visionary of the
time was the Swiss architect known as Le
Corbusier (1887- 1965). Le Corbusier thought
big; he drew plans for vast urban landscapes.

His vision was of an environment populated
by tower blocks in an empty countryside
cut by highways. In hindsight, if you look at
Le Corbusier's modernist plans alarm bells
ring. Le Corbusier's world was one of cars
and concrete. He seemed to forget that real
people would live in these landscapes.

By the 1960s 'free flow traffic design' – as
seen in the USA and Germany – was all the
rage. The concept was that cars would travel
unimpeded by pedestrians. Underpasses,
overpasses and elevated walkways became an
integral feature of the new urban landscape. In
Bristol plans were produced along these lines,
first for the development of the Redcliffe area
and then Lewins Mead and Rupert Street.

The shadow of the wrecking ball loomed
large. A dual carriageway – which required
the demolition of the historic Shot Tower –

HOW TALL?
- Bristol's tallest structures -

- **Cabot Tower**, Brandon Hill – 32.5m (107ft).
- **BRI Chimney**, Kingsdown – 60m (196ft).
- **Radisson Blu Hotel** (former Bristol and West Tower), Colston Avenue – 61m (200ft).
- **Beacon Tower**, Bristol Centre – 63m (207ft).
- **Premier Inn** – former Avon House – 64m (210ft).
- **One Redcliffe Street** (former DRG Building) – 64m (210ft).
- **Wills Memorial Building Tower**, Park Street – 65m (215ft).
- **Telecommunications Tower**, Purdown – 70m (230ft).
- **Tollgate House**, Newfoundland Road – 77m (252ft). (Demolished 2006.)
- **Castlemead** (on edge of Cabot Circus) – 80m (262ft).
- **St Mary Redcliffe Church** – 89m (292ft).
- **Castle Park View** – 98 m (323ft).

Tallest building in the UK – The Shard, London, 310m (1,016ft).

Of course, some buildings, like the Wills Memorial Tower, placed on a hill, look disproportionately tall. Cabot tower is, in fact, only a stumpy 32.5m (107ft) tall.

And the miracle is that until 2020 Bristol's tallest structure was a building that was constructed in the 15th century (though rebuilt in 1872) – the spire of St Mary Redcliffe.

Council leaders formally adopted a tall building policy for Bristol in 2005 aimed at protecting important vistas and historical sites. How strong this resolution is remains to be seen. There is always some egomaniac architect or developer wanting to override guidelines and impose their vanity project on the skyline.

Work is currently underway (2022) on a residential tower in the newly established Redcliffe Quarter. It is expected this sky-scraping 'iconic beacon' will become the tallest building in Bristol.

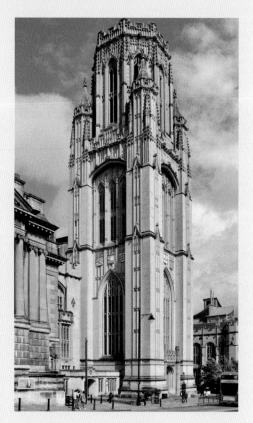

Wills Memorial Building Tower, Park Street – 65m (215ft).

was built on Redcliffe Hill, while a roundabout was constructed yards away from the sublime north porch of St Mary Redcliffe church. Again the schemes foundered before completion. In the Redcliffe area buildings were demolished only to be replaced by temporary car parks, which in turn became permanent car parks.

Progress was quicker at Lewins Mead and Rupert Street, where houses – including a cluster of historic timber framed buildings at the bottom of Christmas Steps – and industrial buildings were cleared and quickly replaced by soul sapping concrete office blocks. Likewise, many of the elegant Georgian terraces linked by steep steps and cobbled pathways on the Kingsdown hillside were demolished with eagerness.[7] To the rear of King Square, three 14 storey slabs fronted by car parks were put up. The economy was buoyant and the white heat of the sixties energy meant that anything seemed possible.

In 1966 plans for inner and outer ring roads were produced which included a proposal that the docks be 'partially reclaimed' i.e. filled in.[8] Also an urban expressway was to cut through historic Queen Square, and cross the docks by Bush House (now the Arnolfini). This was a bridge too far. The planner's utopia was turning into the citizen's nightmare. From now on opposition to the filling-in of the docks, the expensive road schemes and the demolition of much loved buildings was increasingly vocal and well organised. For some areas – such as Easton, and Totterdown where over 500 houses were demolished – the opposition came too late.[9]

In the following years it was shown that free flow traffic through city centres caused as many problems as it solved. 'Easy in' meant 'easy out'. Cities began to suffer from the 'hole in the doughnut effect' whereby businesses and retailers moved to out-of-town locations. Not to mention the dangers of pollution.

The 'stairway to nowhere' was part of a network of pedestrian decks around Lewins Mead and Rupert Street. It was a relic of the planning experiments of the 1950s and 1960s from which many towns and cities continue suffer. It personified out of control planners. When the 1966 plan was drawn-up the planners disdainfully locked themselves away while they dreamt up Bristol's future. They consulted nobody but themselves.

While the car may not, as yet, have been toppled from its throne at least the emphasis these days is on traffic limitation. The fight, however, for pedestrians and cyclists to have equal rights with car drivers continues.

The unexpected benefits of a large scale fire

Large scale fires naturally necessitate a complete reconstruction. After the Great Fire of 1666, London was rebuilt by Christopher Wren on a grand and elaborate scale. The old half timbered, higgledy-piggledy houses had been reduced to ashes. The new streets were wider, the new brick or stone buildings more imposing and graceful. Fortunately, or not, Bristol had escaped such large scale devastation. Until the Second World War, that is.

A SURPRISINGLY COMPLEX SCIENCE

- Street names -

Names can change over time. Nelson Street was once called Gropecunt Lane, an earthier version of the more familiar Lovers Lane. It later became Hallier Lane and, by 1808, in commemoration of the Battle of Trafalgar (1805), was renamed Nelson Street.

In 1969 Mr H.C.W. Harris, Housing Manager and Secretary to the City and County of Bristol wrote a slim volume on the origin of road and flat names used in Bristol. Mr Harris gave an insight into the surprisingly complex science of street naming:

'... *the most important condition is that the name should be euphonious, i.e. will come easily off the tongue. For that reason it will be noticed that the majority of selections are polysyllabic; have more than one syllable. Probably three is ideal, although occasionally monosyllabic names have been adopted where they are particularly suitable. It will also be noted that, with three exceptions, no name of a living person has been used* ...' Harris hastily added, with a tone of relief, that, '... *two of those three are now deceased.*'.

Street names are frequently used to celebrate and instil collective memory. This can cause controversy when history is re-assessed. If, in the past, a street had been named after someone called Shipman or Savile, there might today be demands to change it. How long can Colston Street, Colston Parade and Colston Avenue – all late 19th century creations – remain?

A number of themes emerge in the naming of roads on the new council estates of the 1930s. In Horfield there was a literary trend with:

Ruskin Grove
Shakespeare Avenue
Sheridan Road
Thackeray Walk
Wordsworth Road

While in Lockleaze the preference went towards artists; some of them now out of fashion and forgotten.

Constable Road
Landseer Avenue
Flaxman Close
Romney Avenue
Bonnington Square
Hogarth Walk
Morris Road

Meanwhile, over in Knowle West, the city's cultural aspirations were hijacked by the building contractor, a Mr Murphy, who is said to have insisted on naming the streets he was building after his homeland.

Cavan Walk
Galway Road
Kildare Road
Leinster Avenue

Occasional mistakes have been made. A new road off Horfield Common was to be named Doiran after the First World War battle fought in Bulgaria by the Gloucestershire

A new road off Horfield Common was to be named Doiran, after the First World War battle fought by the Gloucestershire Regiment. Unfortunately, the name was misread by the sign writer, and has been called Dorian Road ever since.

The best street name of all is Cheers Drive, in Speedwell. First suggested as a joke, it was formally adopted in 2020.

Regiment who had their barracks nearby. Unfortunately, the name was misread by the sign writer, and has been called Dorian Road ever since.

And, of course, the best street name of all is Cheers Drive, in Speedwell. First suggested as a joke, it was formally adopted in 2020.

House Numbering

The numbering of houses developed sporadically. House numbering is not just there for your friends, or the postman, to find you. It also allows for people to be taxed, called up for military service, or, even, put under arrest. In 1775, James Sketchely, the author of *The Bristol Directory*, devised and promoted the following system: 'The Exchange is made the centre and every street (a very few excepted) is begun at the end nearest the centre, on the left hand.'[10] This is now the accepted system.

ENDNOTES

1   Boughton, J., *Municipal Dreams*, 2018, Verso, p.61.
2   Anon, *English City. The Story of Bristol.* 1945, J.S.Frys and Son, p.78-9.
3   Ibid., p.86-7.
4   Priest, G. & Cobb, P., *The Fight for Bristol*, 1980, Redcliffe Press, p.12
5   Foyle, A., *Pevesner Architectural Guides - Bristol, 2004*, Yale University Press, p.173.

6   https://www.bbc.co.uk/news/uk-42182497
7   Priest, G. & Cobb, P., op. cit., p.45-50.
8   Bennett, J.B., *Bristol of the Future*, 1966, p.20.
9   Priest, G. & Cobb, P., op. cit., p.71.
10 *Sketchley's Bristol Directory 1775*, Facsimile edition, Kingsmead Reprints, Preface.

TAKE
A WALK

TIME FOR STROLL

- The work of eight major architects in just 200 metres -

(Twenty minutes – easy. Information correct at the time of writing.)

There can be few streets in the country that have such a range of buildings by so many premier 18th, 19th and 20th century architects. Corn Street and Clare Street is a museum of architecture.

Corn Street and Claire Street were once the business centre of Bristol. Here, all the major banks and financial businesses had their offices. Today, these commercial organisations have moved their administrative centres to purpose-built buildings in business parks on the edge of town – or to call centres in India. Many of these beautiful buildings have now been converted to bars and restaurants. These days pints rather than pounds are traded in Corn Street. It is now at night-time that Bristol's once sober commercial heart beats strongest.

This short walk starts at the top of Corn Street at the junction with Broad Street. Begin by admiring the tower of Christchurch ❶

with its quarter jacks – little grey jacketed, moustachioed, figures that strike the quarter hour (currently waiting to be repaired.). Christchurch was re-designed in 1786 by William Paty (1758-1800). The Paty family were a major architectural force in 18th century Bristol. William Paty was the first of the dynasty to be trained in London. He attended

Christchurch with its quarter jacks – little grey jacketed, moustachioed, figures that strike the quarter hour.

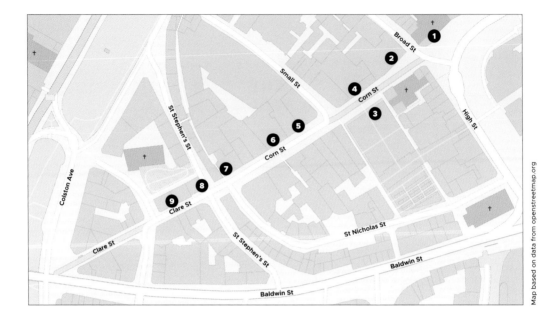

Map based on data from openstreetmap.org

the Royal Academy and is said to have based his design of Christchurch on St Martin-in-the-Fields, London.

Now turn and look at the first building on your right, currently used as the Bristol Register Office ❷. This building, completed in 1827, was originally built as the Bristol Council House by the architect Robert Smirke (1780-1867). A difficult corner site, this unprepossessing building was thought unworthy of the city.

Continue 50 metres. On the left is one of Bristol's best classical buildings, the Palladian style Exchange ❸, by John Wood the Elder (1704-54). Wood was the premier architect of Georgian Bath and was responsible for the world famous Royal Crescent and the Circus. The Exchange was opened in 1743 and was the hub of Bristol's commercial activity during the 18th century. Note that the clock has a third hand – indicating Bristol time. Through the entrance hall is a central courtyard – roofed over in 1870 – with enough space for several dozen traders. The Exchange is now

home to an indoor market and leads to the small shops and the cafes of the adjoining St Nicholas Market. Don't be diverted from your walk – you can return later!

Opposite the Exchange is a Venetian style building that currently houses the Harbour Hotel, ❹ originally, the West of England and South Wales Bank, built by Bristol architects

The first Council House, built in 1552, stood on the corner of Broad Street and Corn Street. It was replaced in 1828 by a new Council House designed by the London-born architect Robert Smirke (1780-1864). This building is now used as a register office.

While the classicist Smirke also built St George (1823), Brandon Hill, he is, perhaps, best known for designing the epic, classical revival building, the British Museum in London.

One of Bristol's best buildings, the Palladian style Exchange, by the John Wood the Elder.

The architect Bruce Gingell is said to have used St Mark's library in Venice as a reference point for this building.

Bruce Gingell (1819-99) and T.R. Lysaght in 1854. Gingell was one of the most progressive Bristol architects of the latter part of the 19th century. He went on to design the General Hospital. Gingell is said to have used St Mark's library in Venice as a reference point for this building. Spend a few moments viewing the sumptuous friezes by John Thomas (1813-62). Thomas was responsible for overseeing the carving on Charles Barry's new Houses of Parliament. On the ground floor the crests of Newport, Bath, Bristol, Exeter, and Cardiff are shown – the main towns from where the bank operated. On the first floor the 'elements and sources of wealth' are symbolised by life-size figures. See if you can spot them. They include: justice and integrity; education and charity; peace and plenty; art and science; navigation and commerce. And above this, chubby cherubs depict the activities of the bank: receiving, paying, storing, coining money, engraving and printing, and trading with Africa and America.

The adornment was intended to emphasize the wealth, and therefore financial stability, of the bank. It didn't stop the bank going bust 20 years later in 1878.

Continue another 50 metres along the street, passing Small Street on your right, until you come to the former Commercial Rooms **5**, now a Wetherspoon's bar. This charming single storey classical building (1809-11) is by the precocious 22-year-old Charles Busby (1788-1834). If you can, go inside and admire the domed roof, the wind dial and the working 100-year-old old gas lamps. Busby went on to have a successful career working in Regency Brighton. The figures on the roof represent (from left to right) Commerce, Bristol and Navigation.

Numbers 37-39 **6** takes us to the 20th century and shows art deco flourishes. The facade is by Sir Giles Gilbert Scott (1880-1960), the architect of Liverpool Cathedral, Battersea Power Station and the designer of the iconic red telephone box. The creamy white stone is Portland stone. As an antidote to the previous worthy sculptures take a moment to admire the frieze above the door of six naked maidens dancing to the figure of Wisdom[1]; a welcome relief from the preachy images we have seen so far.

Continue walking and immediately on your right glimpse down Leonard Lane **7** which

A frieze of six naked maidens dancing to the figure of Wisdom.

Stop at number 27 to enjoy a charming neo-baroque pepper pot gem of 1903 by Sir George Oatley.

Alfred Waterhouse's delightful pink hewed chateau-inspired construction (1899). It was built to house the offices of the Prudential Assurance Company.

follows the course of the medieval town wall.

Corn Street now turns into Clare Street. Again, on your right, stop at number 27 **8** to enjoy a charming neo-baroque pepper pot gem of 1903 by Sir George Oatley (1863-1950), a prolific Bristol architect who, during a career spanning nearly 50 years, also built the Wills Memorial Building at the top of Park Street.

The final building to be admired is Alfred Waterhouse's **9** (1830-1905) delightful pink hewed chateau-inspired edifice (1899) that was built to house the offices of the Prudential Assurance Company. The rough grey slate roof contrasts with the smooth terracotta finish of the building. A keen proponent of the use of multi-coloured tile and brick, Waterhouse was another Victorian great, his supreme achievement being the London Natural History Museum. Waterhouse was commissioned to build over 30 offices for the 'Pru'. Every building was different and designed for each specific site. This one, faced in salmon pink terracotta, is a gem.

You have now completed your tour. Retrace your steps to The Exchange where food and drink awaits to be purchased from the wonderfully eclectic stalls in St Nicholas Market. You've earned it!

ENDNOTES

1   Merritt, D. & Greenacre, F., *Public Sculpture of Bristol*, 2010, Liverpool University Press, p.112.

MAKING HISTORY

RESOURCES THAT HAVE LED THE WAY

- A brief survey of Bristol's historians -

Over the past 250 years, historians and lay people alike have done much groundwork to uncover Bristol's past. The first comprehensive account, *History and Antiquities of the City of Bristol*, was written by William Barrett (1733-89) in 1789.

Barrett, who trained as a surgeon, gathered together early charters and manuscripts. But equally as interesting is his detailed account of Bristol in the 1780s – including descriptions of the docks, industries, markets and fairs. His 700-page tome was accompanied by 30 copperplate illustrations and a specially commissioned large fold-out map. Unfortunately, Barrett is primarily remembered for being duped by the boy poet Thomas Chatterton, who provided bogus information.

It was a good, if flawed start. Forty years later, school teacher and clergyman Samuel Seyer (1757-1831), aware of Barrett's failings, was more rigorous in his approach.[1] Seyer transcribed the raw material of charters, calendars and minute books for his two volume

In 40 years Redcliffe have published over 200 books on the city – many superbly illustrated by Stephen Morris.

Memoirs, Historical and Topographical, of Bristol and its Neighbourhood, (1821-23). Clearly written, reliable, and typographically accessible, Seyer laid out the corpus of Bristol's history from which much further interpretation has flowed. Seyer is one of my first 'go to' historians. His text is accompanied by fine engravings by Edward Blore (1787-1879) with whom he had a difficult relationship.

'Engravers are men of strange manners,' Seyer commented.[2] One wonders what Blore made of Seyer, who was notoriously free with his use of the cane.

At the same time, John Evans (1774-1828), a printer, published *A Chronological Outline of the History of Bristol* (1824). This shorter volume covers much the same ground as Seyer, but in less detail. Financially the book was a failure. Evans sustained a great loss from the publication of the book. The Corporation voted him £20 on delivery of four copies.[3] Evans died in London in 1828 when a theatre which he was attending collapsed on the audience.

Another renowned chronicler was John Latimer (1824-1904), a journalist who worked for the *Bristol Mercury*. His four volume *Annals of Bristol* is an impressive compendium of 17th, 18th and 19th century events. Latimer scanned the newspapers and summarised the major stories. His *Annals* are well researched, but also nicely partial! A classic.

Other go-to Victorian historians are librarians James Fawkner Nichols (1818-83) and John Taylor (1829-93). Their wide-ranging three volume *Bristol Past and Present* is divided into: Civil History (1881); Ecclesiastical History (1881) and Civil and Modern History (1882).

At the beginning of the 20th century, Bristol printers and publishers J. W. Arrowsmith hit gold. Although their main business was printing timetables, they also published the occasional novel. Their most celebrated books were the timeless *Three Men in a Boat* and *The Diary of a Nobody*. But alongside these comedy classics Arrowsmith's produced a

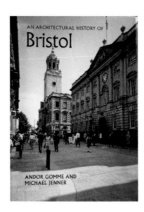

Bristol – an architectural history (1979) by Gomme, Jenner and Little is encyclopaedic and reliable. An updated version by Gomme and Jenner was published in 2011.

range of helpful Bristol guides and directories. Their *Dictionary of Bristol* (1906) provides a comprehensive portrait of the city in the 1900s, while *Bristol and its Famous Associations* (1907) by Stanley Hutton detailed a range of biographical cameos. Arrowsmith's continued to provide updated city guides throughout the 20th century.

There are a number of long standing local history societies and groups that produce publications. Bristol and Gloucestershire Archaeological Society is a venerable organisation going back to the end of the 19th century. Primarily concerned with archaeological excavations, their annual *Transactions* also contain original historical research relating to Bristol. The *Transactions* have recently been digitised and are now word-searchable.

The Bristol Record Society, established in 1928, aims to study, transcribe and publish original manuscripts. The range – from the essential charters to the more mundane, but equally revealing, house inventories – is eclectic and always interesting. Produced annually, these books, with their simple off-white covers, provide an invaluable and readily accessible collection of source material accompanied by knowledgeable analysis.

Scholarly brochures have also been produced by the Bristol Branch of the Historical Association. Between 1960 and 2006 the BBHA produced 120 short monographs. Covering everything from pre-history to the Open-air schools, they are invariably comprehensive, scrupulously researched and peer-reviewed. Well worth checking out. Again, they have been digitised and can be found on-line.

In the 1970s, Redcliffe Press published its first book, *Children's Bristol* (1976). Read as much by adults as children, its runaway success paved the way for Redcliffe's extensive coverage of Bristol's history and built environment. In 40 years Redcliffe have published over 200 books on the city – many superbly illustrated.

When it comes to the built environment, Bristol is well-served with commentaries. The Georgian architecture of Bristol has been extensively covered. C.F.W. Dening, a distinguished architect himself, produced the sumptuously illustrated *Eighteenth Century Architecture of Bristol* (1923), while Walter Ison expanded on this in his *Georgian Buildings of Bristol* (1952). Timothy Mowl's *To Build a Second City* (1991) is witty and opinionated. Andrew Foyle updated Nikolaus Pevsner's ground-breaking, but rather arid, *Buildings of England – North Somerset and Bristol* (1958) with a splendidly illustrated pocket volume (2004). But, for me, *Bristol – an architectural history* (1979) by Gomme, Jenner and Little is encyclopaedic and reliable. An updated version by Gomme and Jenner was published in 2011. Anything written about architecture by Mike Jenner is eminently readable.

For a visual record of Bristol in the 20th century Reece Winstone's distinctive self-published volumes are an unrivalled photographic record of the changing city.

Times change and viewpoints shift. Just as history is written by the victors, so also is it a product of its time. By the 1980s Bristol's history was being re-evaluated and the largely Victorian narrative reassessed. The glories of previous ages were not so glorious after all. The mythologizing of Edward Colston is a case in point. Historians began to highlight Bristol's unpalatable role in the trans-Atlantic triangular

The publishing collective *Bristol Broadsides* gave voice to the previously unheard.

trade and how its colonial links brought great wealth to the city.

There was also an increasing interest in working class history. In the 1980s, the publishing collective *Bristol Broadsides* gave voice to the previously unheard. Many of Bristol Broadsides's booklets came out of history workshops run, in conjunction with the WEA, on council housing estates. The ground-breaking *Bristol's Other History* (1983) contained chapters on labour struggles, woman's emancipation, people's housing and tales of everyday domestic and working life. This was followed by *Placards and Pin Money* (1986) which included Madge Dresser's influential *Black and White On The Buses*, detailing the 1963 Bristol bus boycott.

Publications from the Bristol Radical History Group, formed in 2006, continue this tradition. Although the group's roots are exhilaratingly radical, veering on the anarchic, their publications are scrupulously researched and well worth reading.

In 1997, the establishment of *Regional*

History Centre at the University of the West of England confirmed local history had come of age. The centre has published a number of lavishly illustrated books in partnership with Redcliffe Press and also produces the *Regional Historian* (now an annual yearbook).

But where are the women? This is what Jane Duffus asked, and answered, in her magnificent two volumes of *The Women Who Built Bristol* (2018-19).

There are, of course, many more resources for the Bristol historian. Special mention must go to *Know Your Place* (www.kypwest.org.uk/) a truly fascinating, ever growing, on-line database of maps and heritage information. Established in 2011, rarely a day goes by when I don't consult this addictive digital mapping resource.

These are just some of the resources that have led the way or have personally resonated. And I haven't even mentioned the uniquely

But where are the women? This is what Jane Duffus asked, and answered, in her magnificent two volumes of *The Women Who Built Bristol. (Photo: Jon Craig)*

well-stocked Bristol Central Reference Library - where you should find these publications - and the unrivalled Bristol City Archive for original research.

ENDNOTES

1   Seyer, S., *Prospectus of Memoirs Historical and Topographical*, 1821.
2   Blore began his career as an engraver but was later to become a much respected architect. Among many other works, he extended parts of Buckingham Palace. He was also appointed as official surveyor to Westminster Abbey.

3   Hudleston, C. R., *John Evans of Bristol*, 1939, Bristol and Gloucestershire Archaeological Society, Vol 61, p.196 -201.

SOURCES

A Fellow of Queens College in Oxford, *The Sieges of Bristol in the Civil War*, 1868, Lewis and Taylor.

Abercrombie, P. & Brueton, B., *Bristol and Bath Regional Planning Scheme*, 1930, University Press Liverpool.

Alexander, J. & Binski, P., (Ed) *Age of Chivalry*, 1987, Royal Academy of Arts.

Andrews, A. & Pascoe, M., *Clifton Suspension Bridge*, 2008, Broadcast Books.

Anon, *Bristol as WE remember it*, undated, Bristol Broadsides.

Anon, *Council House Bristol 1956*, Bristol. Unpaginated commemorative brochure.

Anon, *Early Bristol Newspapers*, 1956, Corporation of Bristol.

Anon, *Bristol and Its Environs*, 1875, London.

Anon, *Bristol Bombed*, 1943, F.G Warne.

Anon, *English City. The Story of Bristol.* 1945, J.S.Frys and Son.

Anon, *How to see Bristol*, 1910, Arrowsmith.

Anon, *The Northern Foul Water Interceptor*, undated brochure (1994?), Bristol.

Arrowsmith Ltd, *Official Guide to the City of Bristol*, 1921.

Aughton, P., *Bristol – A People's History*, 2003, Carnegie Publishing.

Backwith, D. and Ball, R., *Bread or Batons*, 2012, Bristol Radical History Pamphleteer Pamphlet #19.

Ball, R., Parkin, D. and Mills, S., *100 Fishponds Road. Life and Death in a Victorian Workhouse.* 2016. Bristol Radical History Group, p.104.

Barton, M., *Dizzy Heights*, in *Bristol Review of Books*, Issue 13.

Beeson, A., *Bristol Central Library and Charles Holden.* 2006, Redcliffe.

Belsey, J and Reid, H., *West at War*, 1990, Redcliffe, Bristol.

Belshaw, G. & Green, R., *Charles Heal and Son's Big Shows*, 2019.

Bennett, J.B., *Bristol of the Future*, 1966.

Bettey, J., *William Worcestre –The Topography of Medieval Bristol*, 2000, Bristol Record Society, Vol 51.

Bettey, J.H., *Bristol Observed*, 1986, Redcliffe Press.

Bishop, J., *Bristol through Maps*, 2016, Redcliffe.

Blackburn, R., *The Overthrow of Colonial Slavery 1776 -1848*, 1988, Verso.

Bolton, D., *Made in Bristol*, 2011, Redcliffe Press.

Boughton, J., *Municipal Dreams*, 2018, Verso.

Branigan.K., *The Romans in the Bristol Area*, 1969, Bristol Branch of the Historical Association.

Briggs, A., *A Social History of England*, 1983, Weidenfeld and Nicolson.

Bristol City Planning and Public Works Committee, *Bristol of the Future*, 1967, Bristol.

Bristol Times and Mirror, *Work in Bristol*, 1883.

British Association. *Bristol and its Environs.* 1875, J Wright and Co.

Broda, C., *Symes Avenue: Building on the Past*, 2008.

Brodie, A., Croom, J. and Davies, J. *Behind Bars*, 1999, English Heritage.

Buchanan, R.A. & Williams, M., *Brunel's Bristol*, 1982, Redcliffe Press.

Buchanan, R.A., *The Industrial Archaeology of Bristol*, 1967, Bristol Branch of the Historical Association.

Burton, E. and Manson, M., *Vice and Virtue. Discovering the story of Old Market.* 2015, Bristol Books.

Butcher, E.E., *Bristol Corporation of the Poor 1696-1898*, 1972, Bristol Branch of the Historical Association.

Caldicott, R.L., *The Life and Death of Hannah Wiltshire*, 2017, Bristol Radical History Group.

Carpenter, M. *The Indifferent Horseman*, 1954, Elek Books.

Clark, G. T., *Report to the General Board of Health*, 1850, For Her Majesty's Stationery Office.

CLASS *Miner's Memories*, 1984?, Adult Studies Department, South Bristol Technical College.

Cottle, B., *Chatterton*, in Ed McGrath, P., *Bristol in the 18th Century*, 1972, David and Charles.

Defoe, D., *A Tour Through the Whole Island of Great Britain*, 1724-6, Penguin Edition 1978.

Dening, C.F.W. *Old Inns of Bristol*, 1943, Bristol.

Diaper, S. in Harvey, C. & Press, J., Ed, *Studies in the Business History of Bristol*, 1988, Bristol Academic Press.

Drake, F. and D'Arpino, T., *Trees of Bristol*, Redcliffe Press, 2014.

Dresser, M. & Giles, S. *Bristol and Transatlantic Slavery*, 1999, Bristol Museums and Art Gallery.

Dresser, M., *Black and White on the Buses*, 1986. Bristol Broadsides.

Dresser, M., Jordan, C. & Taylor, D., *Slave Trade Trail*, 1998, Bristol Museums and Art Gallery.

Dresser, M., *People's Housing in Bristol 1870-1939* in *Bristol's Other History*, 1983, Bristol Broadsides.

Duffus, J. *The Women Who Built Bristol*, 2018, Tangent.

Duffus, J. *The Women Who Built Bristol*: Volume Two. 2019, Tangent.

Evans, J., *A Chronological Outline of the History of Bristol*, 1824, Bristol.

Fedden, M., *Bristol Bypaths*, 1955, Bristol (?).

Fleming, P. & Costello, K., *Discovering Cabot's Bristol*, 1989, Redcliffe.

Fowler, P.J., *Hill-Forts, A.D. 400-700*, in ed. Jesson, M. and Hill, D. *The Iron Age and its Hill-Forts*, 1971, University of Southampton.

Foyle, A. & Pevsner, N., *Somerset: North and Bristol*, 2011, Yale University Press.

Foyle, A., *Pevesner Architectural Guides – Bristol, 2004*, Yale University Press.

Franklin, M., *Prisoners of War in Bristol* - Extracts from the Public Records Office, Greenwich, unpublished manuscript, Bristol Central Reference Library, B30152.

Fuller, T., *History of the Worthies of England, Vol. 2*, 1840, London.

Gage, S. in Duffus, J., *The Women Who Built Bristol*, 2018, Tangent.

Garfield,S., *Just My Type*, 2010, Profile Books.

Ginsell, L.V., *Prehistoric Bristol.* Bristol Branch of the Historical Association, 1969.

Gomme A, Jenner M and Little B: Bristol, *An Architectural History: Bristol*, 1979, Lund Humphries.

Gomme, A. and Jenner, M., *An Architectural History of Bristol*, 2011, Oblong Creative.

Gough, P., *That Vile Place*, Bristol Review of Books. Issue 1, Summer 2006.

Groom, N., *The Death of Chatterton*, in Heys, A. *From Gothic to Romantic: Thomas Chatterton's Bristol*, 2005, Redcliffe Press.

Hall Ellis, M.J., *The Early Years of the Telephone Service in Bristol 1879-1931*, 1985?, British Telecommunications Ltd.

Harrison,T., *Living through the Blitz*, 2010, Faber & Faber.

Harvey, C. & Press, J., Ed, *Studies in the Business History of Bristol*, 1988, Bristol Academic Press.

Holmes, R., *Coleridge – Darker Reflections*. 1998, Harper Collins.

Horton, B., *West Country Weather Book*, 1995, Bristol.

Hunt, S., *Yesterday's To-morrow*, 2012, Bristol Radical Pamphleteer Pamphlet.

Hutton, S., *Bristol and its Famous Associations*, 1907, Arrowsmith.

Ison, W., *The Georgian Buildings of Bristol*, 1952, Faber & Faber.

Jenkins, S., *England's Thousand Best Houses*, 2004, Penguin.

Jenner, M., *Bristol's 100 Best Buildings*, 2010, Redcliffe.

Jones, P., *Canon's Marsh – The Rise and Fall of the Tobacco Bonds*, 1988, Redcliffe Press.

Kelly, A., *Queen Square Bristol*, 2003, Redcliffe.

Kelly, M., *Homes for Heroes 100 – Book of Walks*, 2019, Bristol Cultural Development Partnership.

Lambert, D., *Historic Public Parks – Bristol*. 2000, Avon Gardens Trust.

Lamoine, G., *Bristol Gaol Delivery Fiats 1741-1799*, 1989, Bristol Record Society.

Large, D. and Round, F., *Public Health in Mid-Victorian Bristol*, 1944, Bristol Branch of the Historical Association.

Latimer, J., *Annals of Bristol – Seventeenth Century*, 1900, Georges.

Latimer, J., *Annals of Bristol – Eighteenth Century*, 1893, Bristol.

Latimer, J., *Annals of Bristol – Nineteenth Century*, 1887, Bristol.

Legg, R., *Steepholm – Allsop Island*, 1992, Wincanton.

Lock, G. and Relston, I.. *Atlas of Hillforts of Britain and Ireland* [On Line]. https://hillforts.arch.ox.ac.uk/

Lord, J. & Southam, J., *The Floating Harbour*, 1983, Redcliffe Press.

Lowery, H., *Bristol Review of Books*, Issue 3, Spring 2007.

Malpass, P. & King, A. *Bristol's Floating Harbour: The First 200 Years*. 2009, Redcliffe.

Malpass, P. & Walmsley, J., *100 Years of Council Housing in Bristol*, 2005, Faculty of the Built Environment, University of the West of England.

Malpass, P., *The Bristol Dock Company, 1803 -1848*, 2010, ALHA Booklet,

Manson, M., *Bristol Beyond the Bridge*, 1988, Redcliffe Press.

Manson, M., *Riot! The Bristol Bridge Massacre of 1793*, 1997, Past & Present Press.

Manson, M, *The Hidden History of St Andrews*, Bristol, 2008, Past & Present Press.

Martin, M., *Managing the Poor* in *The Making of Modern Bristol*, ed. Dresser, M. and Ollerenshaw. P., Redcliffe, 1996.

Mason, E. J. *The Horsefair Cemetery, Bristol* in *Transactions of the Bristol and Gloucestershire Archaeological Society* 1957.

Matthews, W. Bristol Directory, 1793, Bristol, (facsimile edition).

Merritt, D. & Greenacre, F., *Public Sculpture of Bristol*, 2010, Liverpool University Press.

Morris, J., *Domesday Book – Somerset*, 1980, Phillimore.

Morton, M.V., *In Search of England*, 1929, Methuen and Co.

Moss, F., *City Pit*, 1986, Bristol Broadsides.

Mount, H., *A Lust for Window Sills*, 2008, London.

Muthesius, S., *The English Terrace House*, 1982, Yale University Press.

Nichols, G., *Clifton and Durdham Downs: A Place of Public Resort and Recreation*, 2006, Bristol Branch of the Historical Association.

Nicholls, J.F. & Taylor,J., *Bristol Past and Present, Volume 1*, 1881, Arrowsmith.

Nicholls, J.F. & Taylor,J., *Bristol Past and Present, Volume 2*, 1881, Arrowsmith.

Odery Symes, J., *A Short History of the Bristol General Hospital*, 1932, Bristol.

Ollerenshaw, P., *The Development of Banking in the Bristol Region, 1750-1914*, in *Studies in the Business History of Bristol*,1988, ed. Harvey, C. & Press, J., Bristol Academic Press.

Penny, J., *All The News That's Fit To Print*, 2001, Bristol Branch of the Historical Association.

Penny, J., *Bristol at War*, 2002, Breedon Books Publishing Co Ltd.

Penrose, S. *Images of Change*, 2007, English Heritage.

Platt, C., *The English Medieval Town*, 1979, Granada.

Poole, S. & Rogers, N., *Bristol from Below*, 2017, Boydell Press.

Porter, R., *English Society in the Eighteenth Century*, 1990, Penguin Books.

Powell, K.G. *The Marian Martyrs and the Reformation in Bristol*, 1972, Bristol Branch of the Historical Association.

Powell, R., *Brunel's Kingdom*, 1985, Watershed.

Priest, G. & Cobb, P., *The Fight for Bristol*, 1980, Bristol Civic Society and Redcliffe Press.

Priest, G., *The Paty Family*, 2003, Redcliffe.

Pudney. J., *Bristol Fashion*, 1960, Putnam.

Quin, P., *The Holy Wells of Bath And Bristol Region*, 1999, Logaston Press.

Ralph, E. *Government of Bristol 1373-1973*, 1973, Bristol Corporation.

Ralph, E., *The Streets of Bristol*, 2001 (Reprint), Bristol Branch of the Historical Association.

Reid, H. *Bristol & Co*, 1987, Redcliffe Press.

Reid, H., *Bristol Blitz. The Untold Story*, 1988, Redcliffe.

Report of the Visiting Justices into the Gaol and Bridewell of the City of Bristol, 1841.

Sanger, 'Lord' G., *Seventy Years a Showman*, 1952, Dent.

Seyer, S., *Memoirs Historical and Topographical of Bristol*, 1823, Bristol.

Sherborne, J., *The Port of Bristol in the Middle Ages*, 1971, Bristol Branch of the Historical Association.

Sherborne, J., *William Canynges 1402-1474*. 1985, Bristol Branch of the Historical Association.

Sketchley's Bristol Directory 1775, Facsimile edition, Kingsmead Reprints.

Smith, P. in Kelly, M.,(ed.) *Homes for Heroes100 – Council Estate Memories*, 2019, Bristol Festival of Ideas,

South Gloucestershire Mines Research Group, *Kingwood Coal*, 2008.

Steeds, M. & Ball, R., *From Wulfstan to Colston*, 2020, Bristol Radical History Group.

Stephenson, P., *Diary of a Black Englishman,* 2011, Tangent Books.

Taylor, W.E., *The Bristol Orphan Houses*, 1871, Morgan & Scott.

Tombs, R.C., *The Bristol Post*, 1899?, Arrowsmith.

Tratman, E.E., *The Prehistoric Archaeology of the Bristol Region* in *Bristol and Its Adjoining Counties,* 1955, Bristol.

Vear, L., *South of the Avon*, 1978, self published, Wotton-Under-Edge.

Vinter, D., *Prisoners of War near Stapleton Road, Bristol.* 1956, Bristol and Gloucester Archaeological Society -Transactions 1956.

Waite, V., *The Bristol Hotwell* in *Bristol in The Eighteenth Century.* 1972, David and Charles.

Waldron, M., *Lactilla, Milkwoman of Clifton*, 1996, University of Georgia Press.

Walker D., *Bristol in the Early Middle Ages*, 1971, Bristol Branch of the Historical Association.

Walters, W., *The Establishment of the Bristol Police Force*, 1975, Bristol Branch of the Historical Association.

Warne, F.G., *Bristol Bombed*, 1943, F.G. Warne.

White, K. & Gallop, R., *A Celebration of the Avon New Cut*, 2006, Fiducia Press.

Whitfield, M., *The Bristol Microscopists and the Cholera epidemic of 1849, 2011*, Avon Local History and Archaeology.

Whittingham, S. *Sir George Oatley*, Redcliffe Press, 2011, P.187-91.

Winstone, R., *Bristol in the 1940s*, 1961, self-published

Witt,C., *The Bristol Bottlemakers*, 3 June 1978, Chemistry and Industry.

Witt,C., Weedon, C., and Schwind, A.P. *Bristol Glass*, Redcliffe Press.

Witts, C, *Tales of the River Severn*, 1998.

Wood, J., *A Description of the Exchange of Bristol*, 1745, Bath (Facsimile edition).

Yorke, T., *Georgian and Regency Houses Explained*, Countryside Books.

Young, C., *The Making of Bristol's Victorian Parks* in *The Transactions of the Bristol and Gloucestershire Archaeological Society,* Volume 116, 1998.

http://british-police-history.uk/show_nav.cgi?force=bristol_river&tab=0&nav=alpha. Accessed 22/02/2020

http://british-police-history.uk/show_nav.cgi?force=bristol_river&tab=0&nav=alpha. Accessed 22/02/2020

http://www.rediffusion.info/Bristol/ Accessed 03/05/2020.

http://www.rediffusion.info/Bristol/ Accessed 03/05/2020.

https://cardiffharbour.com/flatholm/#1488978342717-6b6c84df-5158 Accessed 15/02/2020.

https://cotswoldarchaeology.co.uk/excavation-of-a-roman-villa-complex-in-lockleaze/ Accessed 9/12/2019.

https://en.wikipedia.org/wiki/Bristol_Post Accessed 03/05/2020

https://en.wikipedia.org/wiki/Bristol_Post Accessed 03/05/2020

https://en.wikipedia.org/wiki/Colin_Pillinger 06/05/2020

https://historicengland.org.uk/listing/the-list/list-entry/1201988. 01/06/2020.

https://historicengland.org.uk/listing/the-list/list-entry/1203910. Retrieved 19 November 2019.

https://sounds.bl.uk/Accents-and-dialects/Millenium-memory-bank/021M-C0900X00510X-2600V1

https://www.avonandsomerset.police.uk/about/history-of-the-force/ Accessed 05/01/2020.

https://www.avonandsomerset.police.uk/about/history-of-the-force/ Accessed 05/01/2020.

https://www.bbc.co.uk/history/ww2peopleswar/stories/60/a5382560.shtml 26 April 2020.

https://www.countyasylums.co.uk/barrow-hospital-barrow-gurney/

https://www.countyasylums.co.uk/history/

https://www.merchantventurers.com/ Accessed 19/02/2020.

https://www.slavevoyages.org/ Slave Voyages Database. https://www.ucl.ac.uk/lbs/person/view/45909 Legacies of Slave Ownership database.

I must give a special mention to the digital mapping website, *Know Your Place*. Rarely a day of writing went by without consulting this magnificent and visionary resource.

PICTURE CREDITS

Unless otherwise stated, photographs and illustrations are from the author's collection. We are most grateful to the Bristol Post and Bristol Culture and Creative Industries for permission to use images from their collections.

The images kindly provided by Bristol Archives are noted opposite along with their respective catalogue Reference Numbers.

p11 RefNo: 17563/1/84
p33 left, RefNo: 43207/9/29/77
p57 top, RefNo: 43207/9/19/14

ACKNOWLEDGEMENTS

The *Bristol Miscellany* has been a long time in the making.

We are fortunate in Bristol that we are blessed with the miles of books and research already undertaken on our unique city.

We've also been privileged in Bristol to have some great publishers – it is largely thanks to them that Bristol's history has been made so accessible

Every time I visit Bristol Archives I marvel that we have access to such treasures. The same goes to Bristol Reference Library. And, of course, these places are staffed by the most knowledgeable people.

We are also privileged to have so many passionate experts ready to share their knowledge and learning. Many people have helped and advised me on this project. Academics, amateur historians, dilettantes and interested individuals have all offered information and advice. In no particular order I would like to thank them for so generously contributing time, expertise and enthusiasm.

My heartfelt thanks go to:

- The fabled Richard Jones, unflagging supporter of creative endeavours in Bristol.
- Mark Steeds, erudite pub landlord.
- Trevor Coombs from the Bristol Museum and Art Gallery for his support and advice with regards illustrations.
- Eugene Byrne from the *Bristol Post*, a mine of information, always beautifully told.
- Housing hero Paul Smith.

- Ed 'the Shirt' Hall for information on ferries.
- Railway gurus Andy Gibb (not that one) and Steve Ehrlicher.
- Peter Floyd MBE for comments on the 1966 development plan.
- Barry Horton, the Bristol weatherman.
- Gordon 'Mr Blue Plaque' Young for information on *Lactilla*.
- The inspirational Jane Duffus whose recent books have brought Bristol's women out of the shadows.
- The Bristol Writers Group: Andy Hamilton, Corinne Dobinson, David Griffiths, Piers Marter and Ray Newman for on-going encouragement and advice.
- The legendary Tangent Lunch club: Richard Jones, Beccky Golding, Andy Hamilton, Mark Steeds, Jo Darke, Sol Wilkinson and Nicky Coates for mental sustenance (and laughs);
- Bristol Books Team: Design genius Joe Burt; Clive Burlton; Martin Powell and Richard Jones (again!).
- And all the people of Bristol who make their city so special.

Although I hardly realised it at the time, the Bristol Miscellany was quietly inspired by Maggie Moss. It was a joint project. We explored Bristol together – walking the streets, seeking out old buildings, new corners and forgotten stories. It was the best of times. Without Maggie this book would not have been written. You live on in our hearts, dear Maggs.

INDEX

THE AUTHOR

© Paul Bullivant

Michael Manson studied sociology at Leicester University. He has an MA in Creative Writing from Bath Spa University and a Post Graduate Diploma from Bristol Polytechnic in Local Studies.

Michael was a co-editor of the *Bristol Review of Books* (2006-13), a co-founder of the Bristol Short Story Prize (2008) and an organiser of the Bristol Festival of Literature (2010 - 2020). He currently edits Bristol Civic Society's magazine *Better Bristol*.

Michael is the author of five history books on Bristol:

- *Bristol Beyond the Bridge* (Redcliffe)
- *Riot! The Bristol Bridge Massacre of 1793* (Tangent Books)
- *The Hidden History of St Andrews* (Past & Present Press)
- *Vice and Virtue. Discovering the Story of Old Market, Bristol* (with Dr Edson Burton) (Bristol Books)
- *Manson's Bristol Miscellany Volume 1* (Bristol Books)

Mike has also written three novels. In 2015 his Bristol-based novel *Where's My Money?* was selected by BBC TV as one of their *Books that Made Britain*. The *Jamaica Gleaner* described Mike's most recent novel, *Down in Demerara*, as 'story telling at its best'.

MANSON'S BRISTOL MISCELLANY VOLUME 1

Includes:

- **In the beginning**
  – Hillforts, Romans and Waterpower
- **Power and politics**
  – County limits, churches, chapels, islands in the Bristol Channel, Bristol Castle, walls, gateways and the Society of Merchant Venturers
- **Law and order**
  – The courts, punishment and policing
- **Prisons**
  – Prisoners of war
- **A fractious city**
  – Riots and Bristol Bus Boycot
- **Fire Service**
- **Making money**
  – Markets, fairs and Bristol brands
- **Burden of shame**
  – The triangular trade
- **Bristol's Swansong**
  – Building the Floating Harbour
- **Jolly Colliers**
  – Coal
- **Public Health**
  – Plague, the Hotwell, cess pits, sewers, water supply, and the Downs
- **Hospitals**
  – Bristol's hospitals, psychiatric care and Elizabeth Blackwell
- **What to do with the dead?**
  – Graveyards, cemeteries and bodies for science.